# CILLA BLACK'S

# Blind Date

Photographs by Simon Farrell, Tony Russell, Mike Vaughan.

**DRAGON**

Dragon
An imprint of the Children's Division of the Collins Publishing Group 8 Grafton Street, London W1X 3LA

Published by Dragon Books 1987

Written and compiled by Chris Miller and Gill Stribling-Wright

Designed by Richard Rockwood & David Winpenny

ISBN 0 583 31214 4

Printed and bound in Great Britain by McCorquodale Varnicoat Ltd, Pershore, England

# BIRTH OF BLIND DATE

I was on tour in Australia and I saw this programme which was on telly five days a week based on an American show called "The Dating Game". It was hilarious and I watched it as often as I could.

On the way home, Bobby and I met the kids in Miami for a holiday and all they wanted to do was stay indoors and watch "The Dating Game!" When we got back to London, we had a meeting with Alan Boyd, LWT's then Controller of Entertainment, about "Surprise, Surprise" and I mentioned "The Dating Game" to him and told him that I thought the show would go down really well over here. Alan said that funnily enough, he had bought the rights to the programme and had done a pilot show called "Blind Date", but was wondering who would be the right person to host it.

About half an hour after we'd got home, the telephone went and it was Alan, who said "Bobby, you'll think I'm mad but what about Cilla for Blind Date?" The idea had never entered my head and at first I was a bit worried because I already had one series "Surprise, Surprise" and felt that that was enough. But I agreed and the rest is history . . .

X X

# DIARY OF THE YEAR

SO – HOW DO WE MAKE *BLIND DATE*? WELL, FOR A START, WE
DON'T JUST MAKE IT UP AS WE GO ALONG, YOU KNOW. WE
START WORK MONTHS BEFORE THE SHOW GOES ON AIR...

**DECEMBER**
Nony (Production Secretary) starts sorting through
thousands of applications for next series, files letters,
photos and nails, phones Mummy twice a day etc.

**JANUARY**
Philip (Associate Producer) arrives and locks himself
in a cupboard for a month to think about possible
dates.

Gill (Producer) double-locks cupboard.

**FEBRUARY**
Rosetta (Researcher) sets off to do first interviews in
Newcastle, Plymouth, Aberdeen, Dover and Carlisle
– in that order. *R – Why not buy a map*

Kevin (Associate Producer) comes back after having
a baby. *Work that out!*

St Valentine's Day. No valentines received by BLIND
DATE team. Gloom and despondency all round.

**MARCH**
Philip and Kevin devise dates, write memos, spend
hours on the phone, make coffee. *Yes Nony. Why is this?*

Nony types letters, spends hours on the phone,
doesn't make coffee.

Search party sent out for Rosetta. *Try the Prancing Emu Club LSCT*

**APRIL**
April Fool's Day. Applications received from "Prince
Edward", "Sam Fox", "John Inman" etc.

Anne and Andrea (Researchers), Terry (Director),
Hazel (P.A.) and rest of team assemble. Cries of
"Where's my desk?", "Where's my stapler?" etc.
*And where's my coffee, Nony?*

Auditions start. 200 potential contestants seen in first
week.

Casting of first show. Weather improves now we're
indoors all day.

First studio. Heat wave.

**MAY**
First dates. Weather changes. Temperatures
plummet. Rain and hail.

Studio two.

Fortnightly round of first interviews, auditions,
casting, studio, dates, call-back interviews and
editing begins. *Treadmill, more like*

**JUNE**
*Gill – can the whole team have the 3rd off to go to the Derby? No!*
Studio three.

As above, only more so. *What about Royal Ascot? No!*
Studio four. *Wimbledon? No! No! No!*

As above, only even more so.

**JULY**
*Game, set and match to the Province*
Studio five.

Researchers go out into the country to find
contestants for autumn studios.

**AUGUST**
*Look chaps, instead of sitting on the beach, why don't you recce a few dates? Good bye!*
Summer Hols.

**SEPTEMBER**
Team re-assembles with new Production Secretary
(Karen).

Nony goes on coffee-making course.

Show on air. Even more mail to contend with. *Think team what are we going to do?*

Studio six.

First discussion of Christmas show.

**OCTOBER**
Studio seven. *Come on chaps – ideas please!*

Second discussion of Christmas show.

Studio eight.

**NOVEMBER**
*Sorry, can't make it*
Studio nine.

Christmas show crisis meeting. *No can do.*

Christmas show crisis meeting crisis.

Christmas show crisis meeting crisis meeting. *Be there or be square!*

Christmas show crisis meeting crisis meeting crisis meeting. *—Why?*

**DECEMBER**
Christmas show crisis finally resolved. We will have a
tree.

Studio ten. Christmas show recorded. End of series.

Karen (Production Secretary) starts sorting through
thousands of applications for next series, files letters,
photos and nails, phones Mummy twice a day etc.

And so on and so on and so on...

# HOW TO APPLY

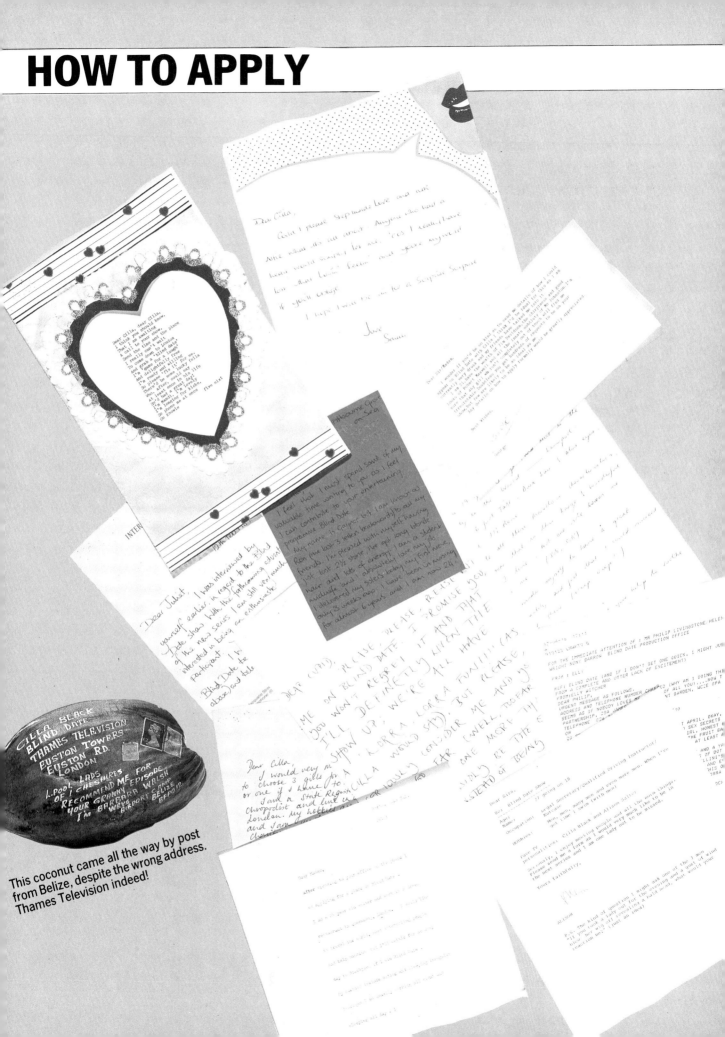

This coconut came all the way by post from Belize, despite the wrong address. Thames Television indeed!

# THE BLIND DATE PERSONALITY TEST

BUT – AND THIS IS A QUESTION YOU CAN ONLY ANSWER YOURSELF – IS <u>BLIND DATE</u> FOR YOU?

WELL, THERE'S ONLY ONE WAY TO FIND OUT, AND THAT'S TO DO OUR SPECIAL <u>BLIND DATE</u> PERSONALITY TEST. THERE ARE 20 QUESTIONS, AND ALL YOU HAVE TO DO IS CHOOSE WHICH ANSWER YOU PREFER TO EACH ONE, AND THEN COUNT UP YOUR "A"S, "B"S AND "C"S AT THE END. OFF YOU GO – AND BE HONEST, NOW!

1   If you could have a fortnight's holiday anywhere in the world, starting tomorrow, where would you go?
    A   A week in Bermuda, followed by a week in Hawaii, with Concorde standing by to take me wherever else I fancied.
    B   Canvey Island.
    C   Florence, to see the art treasures.

2   What do you say when you walk into a room full of people?
    A   "Here I am!"
    B   "Sorry, I didn't mean to butt in or anything, but . ."
    C   "Ah, there you all are!"

3   You have the misfortune to be served a very badly cooked meal in a restaurant. What do you do?
    A   Tip it over the waiter's head.
    B   Eat it, saying to yourself "Well, it wasn't too disgusting really".
    C   Make a discreet complaint to the manager.

4   When you're nervous, do you
    A   Talk a lot, crack a lot of jokes, fizz with energy,
    B   Clam up and say nothing.
    C   Control yourself by will-power and psychological self-mastery?

5   A good friend lets you down on a matter of some importance. What do you do?
    A   Slag them off whenever you get the chance.
    B   Convince yourself it was your own fault.
    C   Tell your friend straight how betrayed you feel.

6   How much do you watch television?
    A   All the time. I've got a wrist TV, so that I can tune in while I'm driving my Porsche.
    B   Frankly, I think it's watching me.
    C   Hardly ever. Personally, I prefer a good book.

7   You've arranged to meet your date at 8 o'clock. When do you show up?
    A   9.30.
    B   4.30.
    C   As near 8 o'clock as you can manage.

8   You're in a group and the others start gossiping about your best friend. Do you
    A   Join in, adding fuel to the flames,
    B   Sit quiet and deny even knowing the person,
    C   Stand up for your friend?

9   You lose a game of tennis against an inferior opponent. Are you
    A   Convinced you were robbed,
    B   Not at all surprised really,
    C   More determined than ever to improve your game?

10   What dog are you most like?
    A   A Dobermann Pinscher.
    B   A lap dog.
    C   It's foolish to try to compare people to dogs. People are people.

11   If your date criticizes the way you're dressed, do you
    A   Point out that you're always in the height of fashion, and anyone who can't see that is an ignorant vulgar nerd,
    B   Burst into tears, then go and change at once,
    C   Try not to show you're hurt by laughing it off, but secretly be disgusted by your date's bad manners?

12   What part of your body do you look at most?
    A   Your face, in the mirror.
    B   Your navel.
    C   None. It's other people I'm interested in.

13   You feel yourself falling in love. Do you
    A   Put a stop to it at once, because all you want right now is a good time,
    B   Just *know* you're going to be humiliated yet again,
    C   Let it happen without going overboard?

14   What job would you most like to do?
    A   Film/rock star.
    B   Assistant Filing Clerk (Grade 9).
    C   Helping those less fortunate than yourself.

15   You win £500 in a raffle. Do you
    A   Blow it all on one wild night out,
    B   Put it in the Post Office,

C Spend some of it, save some of it, and give some of it to charity?

16 You come back into the office and realize everyone is talking about you. What do you do?

A Congratulate them on choosing such a fascinating topic.

B Slink out again and hide in the photocopying room.

C Ignore them and quietly get on with the job you're paid to do.

17 Who are you most likely to tell your troubles to?

A The popular press.

B The goldfish.

C A close friend, or your mother.

18 A horribly embarrassing incident happens at a party. Do you

A Rush round the other rooms, inviting everyone to come and watch,

B Blush and leave,

C Arrange a sing-song in the next room to take people's minds off it?

19 Your current boy/girlfriend introduces you to his/her parents. How do you greet them?

A "Hi, babes!"

B "Don't worry, I'm going in a moment . . ."

C "Good afternoon. How do you do?"

20 Do you see your possible appearance on BLIND DATE as

A The first step on the road to mega-stardom,

B A bit of a worry, really,

C A bit of fun, to be enjoyed, but not taken too seriously?

# WELL, HOW DID YOU GET ON?

## MOSTLY "A"S

I don't know whether you know what the word "poser" means – probably not, after all, it does consist of more than one syllable – but it describes you to a T. You're far too big for your disco' boots. OK, you can dish out criticism, but can you take it? How would your ego cope with being dissected on BLIND DATE? Not very well, perhaps. On the other hand . . . you are brash and lively and confident, and everyone will enjoy seeing you come a cropper. You should apply – and give us all a laugh.

## MOSTLY "B"S

Do you seriously want to be on television? You are a private person – sensitive, cautious and easily hurt. And you put yourself down far too much. Unless, of course, it's all self-mockery. If that's the case, you should apply too. Our very best contestants are those who are prepared to laugh at themselves. Come along, and let us all enjoy your dry wit.

## MOSTLY "C"S

You're too good to be true, but – dare one say it? – aren't you just a teeny little bit boring? Sure, you're observant and intelligent and well-balanced, but honestly, you're far too serious. This is BLIND DATE, not WEEKEND WORLD. Don't be so middle-aged! That said . . . if you can lighten up a bit, you should apply too. We need you. With your insight, you could be just the person to tell that Type "A" wally a few home truths.

SO — LET'S SUPPOSE YOU'VE DECIDED YOU'RE JUST THE SORT OF PERSON WE'RE LOOKING FOR FOR THE SHOW. YOU'VE WRITTEN TO US AND FILLED IN THE APPLICATION FORM WE SENT YOU. WHAT NEXT?

WELL, THE CHANCES ARE THAT NOT A LOT WILL HAPPEN FOR QUITE A LONG TIME. THEN, ONE DAY WHEN YOU'VE COMPLETELY FORGOTTEN YOU EVER APPLIED, YOU'LL GET A PHONE CALL FROM ONE OF OUR RESEARCHERS FIXING UP A FIRST INTERVIEW WITH YOU IN YOUR HOME TOWN. THERE SHE'LL TAKE YOUR PHOTOGRAPH AND ASK YOU SUCH THINGS AS —

**— WHAT DO YOU LIKE ABOUT "BLIND DATE"?**

**— WHY DO YOU WANT TO BE ON THE SHOW?**

**— WHY DO YOU THINK YOU'D MAKE A GOOD CONTESTANT?**

Anne, a researcher, setting off on her travels.

**Richard**

Nony, the Production Secretary, hands out some name tags in reception.

(HOW WOULD <u>YOU</u> ANSWER THOSE QUESTIONS?)

SHE'LL ALSO PROBABLY THROW AT YOU A FEW QUESTIONS OF THE TYPE WE HAVE ON THE SHOW, JUST TO TEST YOUR QUICK-WITTEDNESS — BECAUSE THAT, AFTER ALL, IS WHAT WE'RE LOOKING FOR — THE ABILITY TO THINK ON YOUR FEET AND HAVE FUN.

THEN WHAT? WELL, MORE THAN LIKELY YOU'LL HAVE ANOTHER WAIT AS OUR RESEARCHERS CATCH UP ON THE BACKLOG. AND THEN, RIGHT OUT OF THE BLUE AGAIN, A LETTER WILL PLOP ONTO YOUR DOORMAT ONE MORNING, INVITING YOU TO COME DOWN TO LONDON FOR AN AUDITION. BOYS AND GIRLS ARE AUDITIONED SEPARATELY — FOR OBVIOUS REASONS! — USUALLY IN GROUPS OF ABOUT TEN. RICHARD, WHO HAD TO WAIT AWHILE HIMSELF, TAKES UP THE TALE . . .

"What we did was, we had these name things stuck on us – it was like being at school. Then we walked down the corridors crocodile fashion, and we had a chat and a cup of coffee. There was everyone there, there was, I presume – I didn't know at the time – but I presume there was a producer, a director, researchers and . . . half the team there, I would have thought. And they were just taking notes – it was a bit, you know, it was as if you was being scrutinized constantly . . . and you were. You'd just sort of glance over

Let auditions commence.

# ON BLIND DATE

your right shoulder, and there'd be someone there, giving you the old once-over, up and down, and start scribbling things down, and you're thinking "God, what are they writing?" And you try not to pick your nose, because it was obvious that somebody would see you, with so many people watching! Then we did sort of like a dicky run-through of the game. I think that was basically to assess how sharp we were at answering questions, and I don't think I was too hot at all . . . I think the point of the exercise was to get your brain working, so they could see, you know, how intelligent you were — how you reacted under pressure, really. But I thought 'Well, that's to find out if you're suitable' — and it was necessary . . ."

AND, WHAT'S MORE, NEARLY 300 PEOPLE HAVE SURVIVED THE EXPERIENCE AND GONE ON TO APPEAR IN THE SHOW — INCLUDING RICHARD HIMSELF!

IN FACT, THE AUDITIONS ARE VERY INFORMAL AND RELAXED, PROVIDED YOU CAN ANSWER QUESTIONS LIKE —

Kevin, the Associate Producer, plays the game with Androulla, Sharon and Eve.

— IF YOU WERE A MEMBER OF THE OPPOSITE SEX, WHAT WOULD YOU ENJOY DOING MOST THAT YOU CAN'T DO NOW?

WE GET SOME VERY FUNNY ANSWERS.

FROM THE MEN:

"Have a baby."
"Be Supergran."
"Wear a gold lamé frock."
"Do the washing up . . . it's so fulfilling for women to do household chores."
"Go out with someone like me."
"Book a driving test."
"Be a feminist."
"Get a sugar daddy."

FROM THE WOMEN:

"Play Rugby and be in the scrum."
"Bottom-pinching."
"Shaving."
"Go 15 rounds with Frank Bruno."
"Be a trucker and get dirty."
"Wear a bowler hat and read the *The Financial Times.*"
"Drive a Lamborghini and be a gigolo."
"Drive a Ford Escort with 'Trev' and 'Trace' on the windscreen."

AND THOSE ANSWERS SHOW VERY CLEARLY, I THINK, WHAT TODAY'S BOYS AND GIRLS THINK OF EACH OTHER!
ANOTHER QUESTION WE ASK IS WHICH PUBLIC FIGURES DO THEY THINK THEY MOST RESEMBLE?
THE BOYS SEE THEMSELVES AS . . .

Prince Andrew (the *Spitting Image* version), Madonna ("Because I can't sing"), Arthur Daley, Chris Biggins, Jerry (of Tom and Jerry), J.R. ("Because of his sensitive way of manipulating women") Denis the Menace, Prince Charles ("Because of my ears"), Derek Jameson, Anna Raeburn and "Myself"!

THE GIRLS SEE THEMSELVES AS . . .

George Michael, Margaret Thatcher, Pamela Stephenson, Angie Watts, Lulu, Joan Collins, Annie Lennox, Hilda Ogden, Mick Jagger, Joan Rivers and Felicity Kendal.

BUT NOT A SINGLE CILLA BLACK! I'M QUITE HURT . . .

OCCASIONALLY, JUST FOR FUN, WE EVEN ASK FOR AN ANIMAL IMPERSONATION...

Tim, being a boa constrictor, attacking Rosetta, a researcher.

Bryan being a fly on the wall.

Linda being a kangaroo.

Brigitte being a bird.

THE ACTUAL CASTING OF THE SHOW IS A RATHER COMPLI-
CATED BUSINESS. THERE ARE SO MANY FACTORS TO BE
TAKEN INTO CONSIDERATION . . .

IN AN OFFICE HIGH UP THE LWT BUILDING, THE PRODUC-
TION TEAM IS GATHERED ROUND A DESK ON WHICH ARE
SPREAD DOZENS OF APPLICATION FORMS AND PHOTO-

# CASTING

## EXCEPT . . .

Except that three out of the four of them are from the London area, and we always try to have a good geographical mix. So Shirley from Purley is replaced by Deirdre from Yeovil.

However, that immediately throws up another problem, because both Deirdre and Kirsty have long red hair – in fact, they look terribly similar. So Kirsty is put to one side (better luck next time, Kirsty!) and Shirley from Purley is brought back in again.

Perhaps, though, someone suggests, Shirley is on the wrong side of the screen. With her bubbly personality she'd make a wonderful picker. So Shirley is peeled off for Round One of another show, and her place is taken by Maureen, a hairdresser from Stockport.

Now someone else queries whether Wayne is in the right place. He was very quick and funny in auditions, and he'd be terrific at answering the questions. So Wayne is taken out (to go into Shirley's round?) and replaced by Gwyn, an air steward from Merthyr Tydfil.

The only snag with Gwyn is that he's only 5ft 5ins, and Gina from Walsall is 5ft 10. It's OK if a boy is much taller than a girl, but the other way about looks a bit like a comic turn, and that's not what we want. So Gina is replaced by Brenda from Newcastle, who is Gwyn's size.

Everyone looks at the round. Gwyn choosing from Brenda, Maureen and Deirdre. It looks fine.

Except . . .

*(Cont. at top of opposite page)*

GRAPHS. THEY ARE ATTEMPTING TO CAST ROUND TWO OF A SHOW, IN WHICH A BOY HAS TO PICK ONE OF THREE GIRLS.

LET'S JOIN THEM AS THEY DISCUSS THE POSSIBILITY OF HAVING WAYNE FROM ILFORD PICKING FROM GINA FROM WALSALL, KIRSTY FROM CLAPHAM AND SHIRLEY FROM PURLEY. IT LOOKS OK.

Except that he wouldn't actually get on with any of them! We always try to give the picker at least one person he or she would really like, not because we're looking for a long-term romance or anything – that would be a bonus, of course – but because part of the fun of the game is to see if they choose the one we think is ideal for them (they hardly ever do!)

So, one of the three will have to go and since Maureen really isn't his type at all, it'll have to be her. The girl Gwyn would really get on with, everyone agrees, is Shirley from Purley, and so, although she'd have made a great picker, it's decided to put her back in this round.

The next snag arises when it's discovered that Deirdre is the wrong age group for Gwyn. In her place, someone suggests bringing Kirsty back. She's more or less Gwyn's age, and there's only one other Londoner, so Kirsty it is.

Suddenly, a crisis looms. A check with the other round in this show reveals that the picker there, Lynne, is an air hostess – and Gwyn, of course, is an air steward. It's all beginning to look like an ad. for British Airways. No one wants to disturb Round One, so Gwyn will, reluctantly, have to be put to one side. The search is on for another picker. Who is there? Well, Charlie is very dishy, and it's good to have a picker a girl would really want to be chosen by, but he's probably not confident enought for the job. He wouldn't keep the questions coming. The only suitable person available for the Studio Day in question, it seems, is Wayne from Ilford. Although we'd prefer to have him on the other side of the screen, he'd undoubtedly be a good, strong picker too. So let's have him back in.

There's one more problem. We've now got to give Wayne someone *he*'d get on with. He's sporty and very much the outdoor type, and neither Brenda, Shirley nor Kirsty would claim to be that. The girl who is, out of all those available, is Gina from Walsall. Just his type. They'll have a great day together – if he picks her! In she goes.

So, it's Wayne from Ilford, picking from Gina from Walsall, Kirsty from Clapham and Shirley from Purley. That looks great.

Except . . .

*(Cont. at top of opposite page)*

# PREPARING FOR THE STUDIO

THE SHOWS FOR THE NEXT STUDIO ARE NOW CAST, BUT THERE ARE STILL MANY THINGS FOR THE PRODUCTION TEAM TO DO BEFORE STUDIO DAY. HERE ARE JUST A FEW OF THEM . . .

Karen (Production Secretary).

Nony (Production Secretary).

- Type out Interviews from last filming day ———— production Secretary
- Edit and Cut Interviews on paper ———— Programme Associate Producer
- Telephone Contestants for next studio to let them know they've been cast. Then confirm by letter ———— Researchers/ Production Secretary
- Devise and organize dates ———— Associate Producers/ stage Manager
- select photographs of dates out of previous studio and transfer to Videotape ———— Director
- Book hotels, and flights and other transport for contestants ———— Production Secretary
- Pre Edit: the interviews from filming day are cut together and combined with the photographs to form insert sequences to be dropped into the shows in studio ———— Producer/Director P.A./ Associate Producers/ V.T.R Editor
- Write short biographies of contestants for CILLA ———— Researchers
- script day ———— Writer/Associate Producers
- Book stand by contestants (in case anyone drops out) ———— Researchers
- Type Camera script ———— P. A.
- Telephone contestants to discuss what they are going to wear on the show and check if they have passports ———— Researchers
- Book stand-ins (professional actors who will play the game with contestants during studio rehearsal ———— Stage Manager
- Telephone pickers to talk about their Questions; they are asked to provide at least ten, of which the producer will choose three ———— Programme Associate
- Check lighting and camera crews, especially if new to show ———— Director
- Book dressing room for CILLA and contestants ———— P. A.
- Read Through: CILLA comes in to watch insert sequences from pre-edit and read script ———— CILLA/PRODucer/ writer/Associate Producers/ P.A.
- Type out this List ———— Production Secretary

Philip (Associate Producer), John (Stage Manager) and Kevin (Associate Producer) planning dates.

Terry (Director).

John (Stage Manager).

Andrea (Researcher).

Anne (Researcher).

Hazel (Production Assistant).

# HOW NOT TO DRESS FOR TELEVISION

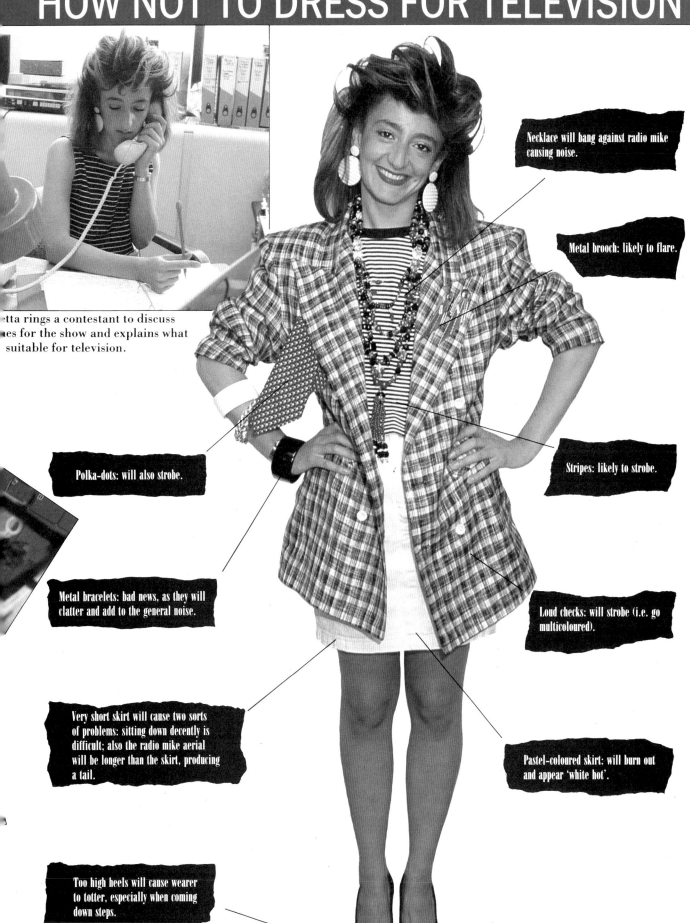

...tta rings a contestant to discuss
...es for the show and explains what
...suitable for television.

Necklace will bang against radio mike causing noise.

Metal brooch: likely to flare.

Polka-dots: will also strobe.

Stripes: likely to strobe.

Metal bracelets: bad news, as they will clatter and add to the general noise.

Loud checks: will strobe (i.e. go multicoloured).

Very short skirt will cause two sorts of problems: sitting down decently is difficult; also the radio mike aerial will be longer than the skirt, producing a tail.

Pastel-coloured skirt: will burn out and appear 'white hot'.

Too high heels will cause wearer to totter, especially when coming down steps.

# THE STUDIO DAY

I SUPPOSE THE QUESTION WE GET ASKED MORE OFTEN THAN ANY OTHER ABOUT **BLIND DATE** IS: "DO THE COUPLES **REALLY** NOT MEET BEFOREHAND?" WELL, NO, BELIEVE IT OR NOT, THEY **REALLY** DON'T – FOR THE VERY GOOD REASON THAT, IF THEY DID, THERE'D BE NO GAME – AND NO FUN!
IN FACT, MOST OF THE TEAM'S ENERGY ON STUDIO DAY IS TAKEN UP WITH MAKING SURE THAT THE PICKERS AND THE PICKEES THEY'RE GOING TO PICK FROM ARE NEVER ANYWHERE NEAR EACH

## HOW TO BE A BLIND DATE PICKER

1) Always make clear which pickee you are speaking to. Identify them by number. Make sure they speak up and understand the questions.

2) Try to form a picture of each pickee from their first answer. This will help you tell them apart later.

3) Follow up their answers if you want to know more.

4) Have fun with Cilla. Ideally, the two of you should be a double act, bouncing off each other (literally, if you must!).

5) When you make your choice, say why and make it clear who you are choosing. Don't change your mind. The audience is liable to shriek after you have made your choice. Don't be unnerved or have second thoughts.

PICKERS' BRIEFING ROOM

THE PICKERS PLAY A PRACTICE GAME.

BRIEFING:
PRACTICE GAMES:
4PM
6PM

THE STUDIO

PICKERS' DRESSING ROOM
CHANGE 5.45 – 6.00PM

LIFT

PICKERS' MAKE-UP ROOM
6.45PM

PICKERS' REHEARSAL 4.45 – 5.45PM

GILL REHEARSING WITH THE PICKERS.

SIMON, THE FLOOR MANAGER, HOLDS A DRESS UP FOR A CAMERA CHECK.

OTHER. THIS IS DONE BY KEEPING THEM LITERALLY AT OPPOSITE ENDS OF THE BUILDING. THEY HAVE THEIR OWN ROOMS WHERE THEY EAT, ARE BRIEFED AND PLAY PRACTICE GAMES, THEIR OWN MAKE-UP ROOMS – EVEN THEIR OWN LIFTS! THE ONLY TWO PLACES BOTH GROUPS GO TO ARE THE DRESSING ROOMS, TO CHANGE, AND THE STUDIO, FOR CAMERA REHEARSAL. WE MAKE ABSOLUTELY SURE (CONFIRMING BY TELEPHONE) THAT THEY'RE NEVER THERE AT THE SAME TIME!

# HOW TO BE A BLIND DATE PICKEE

**DO'S**

1) DO Be yourself (only more so). We've asked you to come on the show because we think you have an engaging personality, so let's see it.

2) DO Speak slowly rather than quickly. If you think you're talking far too slowly, that's probably about right. Take a deep breath before saying anything.

3) DO Try to have a perfectly natural conversation with the picker, even though you can't see him or her.

4) DO Work as a team. The three of you can have a lot of fun helping, competing with and playing off one another.

5) DO Even if you don't get picked, shake hands with or kiss Cilla when you come round the screen. Don't miss Cilla out – it's part of the show she really enjoys!

**DONT'S**

1) DON'T Overdo it or try to be too funny. The flash remark that makes your friends roar their heads off in the pub isn't necessarily appropriate on TV at 6.30 in the evening.

2) DON'T Look for the camera. It's the cameraman's job to find you, not vice versa.

3) DON'T Slouch or scratch or look at your watch. The camera is on you the whole time.

4) DON'T Let the audience stop you if you've something else to say. You don't have to stop just because you've got a laugh or a round of applause.

5) DON'T Forget you've got a brain. Listen carefully to the questions and the other answers, and react accordingly.

PICKEES' DRESSING ROOM
CHANGE 6.30 – 6.45PM

PICKEES' BRIEFING ROOM

ROSETTA BRIEFING THE PICKEES.
2.30PM
4PM

BRIEFING:
PRACTICE GAMES:

LIFT

PICKEES' MAKE-UP ROOM
6.45PM

PICKEES' REHEARSAL 3.00 – 3.45PM

THREE PICKEES, MANDY, SHARON AND CAROL, REHEARSE THE GAME WITH GILL STANDING IN FOR CILLA. QUESTIONS FROM PREVIOUS SHOWS ARE ASKED BY A PROFESSIONAL ACTOR PLAYING THE PICKER.

ZERO HOUR APPROACHES. THE PICKEES ARE TAKEN INTO THE STUDIO AT ABOUT 7.25, READY FOR RECORDING. ONCE THEY ARE HIDDEN, THE PICKERS ARE BROUGHT IN FROM THEIR MAKE-UP ROOM. EVERYONE IS RARING TO GO. BUT FIRST . . .

# MY DAY

"I get the script three days before the studio usually, and then I come in, say, the day before the studio for what we laughingly call the "read through". Sometimes we waste half an hour gossiping about what happened to me last week, and I'm apologising for not having watched the "bish-bash". The "bish-bash", as we call it, means the bit when a couple have been on the date and they come back and are filmed, and we find out what they said about each other. I get a tape of that with the script, and I try to look at it before I go to the read through, so that I can work out my own questions for the couples coming back. Of course, some questions are sorted out for me which, with the script, I "Cillarise", or put in my own words.

We watch the bish-bashes, go through the script, and read the biographies of the Numbers 1s, 2s and 3s etc., and we all muck in – and out of it I get a lot of ideas. But I really can't script my answers, so what you see is what you get!

It's an easy day for me, the preparation day, but the studio day, that's different, particularly if it's on a Monday. I hate doing Blind Date on a Monday, because my Nanny doesn't come back to work on a Monday until after the kids have gone back to school, so I'm up at the crack of dawn, half past six or whatever. Gill, my Producer, tells me that I do a better show when I've been up dead early on a Monday, because I'm so worried that I have so much to do, that I give more than 150%. If the studio is on any other day, it's a different kettle of fish, because I like a good eight hours' sleep, so I don't get up until about nine o'clock, do my hair, 'cos I always do my own hair for Blind Date, and then have a brunch. At about 1.30 pm, LWT very kindly send a car for me and Bobby, 'cos I'm due on the floor, as we call it, the studio floor, at 2.30 in the afternoon.

I do a very quick rehearsal, really it's just for cameras, sound and lighting, and actually I'm not very good at rehear-

sals, I think if you were to see me at rehearsals you'd think "Oh my God, she's going to die." I don't rehearse with the actual kids who are going to be on, I rehearse with actors and actresses pretending to be them. Then I go to my dressing room, and go over my script and the biographies again, and try and remember everyone's name. I'm really terrible at remembering names, and it wasn't my idea, but I'm sure that one of the reasons we call them Numbers 1, 2 and 3 is because there are too many names to remember.

After an hour or so, I do go·and meet the pickers. We do two shows a night, and I don't meet the rest of the kids until the show, but the pickers are hidden away and can't obviously meet the people they will be going on a date with, so I have a little chat and welcome them to the studio. Once they're all relaxed, I go and get my polyfilla on ... I go to make-up! That's usually around 4.30 pm, and after I've got that on, I go back to the dressing room, and I literally interview Bobby. He plays all the parts, and I don't know what I'd

do without him. I interview him like he's been on the date, and he's really very good. After I've done all that, I have a light supper, well, I mean, I just pick at it really, and then all of a sudden it's "check make-up" time, and I change into whatever I'm wearing for the show. I never try on the outfits on the day, only if there's a problem, because I'm so confident with Stephen Adnitt who designs my clothes, and he knows my body so well – I shouldn't say that really! I never thought I could trust a man to do that,

but he's very good right down to the details of brooches and things. Once I'm dressed and ready to go, Bill Martin, our warm-up man, introduces me to the audience and I go on and have a little chat, and sometimes there's somebody in the audience who'll talk to me, and I love it when the audience talks back because it sort of relaxes me. But once I get on the floor, I wanna get on with it, because it's been a long day – I've taken the kids to school, and now I wanna get the show on the road."

Audience now seated, Bill Martin, warm-up man, welcomes them to the studio.

Sound crew fix microphones & transmitters — a ticklish business!

Cilla chats to Stephen backstage as he gives her costume the final once over.

Pickers in another make-up room are waiting nervously.

A last minute make-up check.

The audience are let in!

CP7A  CP9A  CP8B  BK 1

BK 1  CAM1  CAM2

ITV  TX  TX

"Are we nervous? Never!"

Bill hands the mike to Cilla for a quick word with the audience.

Camera and sound crew get in position while...

...the picker waits behind the set.

Cilla has last minute word with Gill while Simon, Floor Manager looks on.

Graham, the Voice, settles down.

"Stand by".

"

I'm a very romantic person. So, if I was the love of your life, how would you react or treat me?

You don't know who I am behind here. If I turned out to be (say) Joan Collins, how would you react?

Sing me a song that tells me something about you.

I've got artistic leanings. Tell me, what is the most artistic thing about you?

Would you be prepared to fight to defend me – and, if you did, would you be any good?

Tell me something about yourself in not more than three words.

I'm a bit unconventional and really go for men of the Woody Allen type. How do you measure up to that ideal?

What is your idea of a really enjoyable Sunday afternoon?

What question were you most afraid I was going to ask you?

How would you go about attracting a girl's attention across a crowded room?

If you could get rid of one thing from your life, what would it be – and why?

I'm very fond of animals. I'd like you to do an impression of the animal you most resemble or think you resemble.

If you wanted to buy me some clothes as a surprise present, how would you go about finding out my size?

What sort of girl would you most want me not to be?

Looking at the other two, what would you say is their worst physical feature?

How would you react if I smashed your new car on the first day you had it?

What is the most macho thing about you?

No.1, tell me frankly what a date with No.2 would be like. No.2, tell me frankly what a date with No.3 would be like. No.3, tell me frankly what a date with No.1 would be like.

What do you look for in a daily newspaper – and what's the first thing you turn to in the morning?

I can usually tell people's characters from their eyes. So – No.1, describe No.2's eyes to me. No.2, describe No.3's eyes to me. And No.3, describe No.1's eyes to me.

Who is your favourite fictional character – and why?

If you saw an attractive looking policewoman on the beat, how would you go about chatting her up?

Suppose you gave me an expensive piece of jewellery and I immediately lost it. How would you react?

What reason would the other two have to be jealous of you?

If you stood in front of a full length mirror, what nickname would you give yourself?

How often do you utter the words "I love you"?

If you shared a flat with two women, what would be your greatest problem be?

If I were Juliet and you were Romeo, how would you get me out onto my balcony in the middle of the night?

What do you hope to be doing in five years' time – and what do you honestly think you will be doing?

My ideal man is Richard Gere. How do you rate yourself from 0-10 against this ideal – and why?

I really don't like untidiness, so, tell me, what is the untidiest thing about you?

Which of the other two would you find it easier to make friends with – and why?

I love dancing. What name would you give to your dancing style?

I often day-dream about being proposed to. How would you propose to me in an unusual and memorable way?

I don't like men with bad manners. Convince me you're a gentleman.

Given a chance, I can be quite extravagant with other people's money. How would you stop me spending yours without giving me the impression you were mean?

Suppose you and I had arranged to hold a dinner party, and then I had to go out all day until just before it was due to start. How would you cope?

If you were going on a rucksack holiday, what would you pack and where would you go?

If you were offered a free magazine subscription for life, which magazine would you choose?

I'm in the P.R. business. Imagine you're a salesman trying to sell yourself to me. What would be your

# GIRLS, SO FAR

opening line?

If you were married, how would you feel about your wife being the breadwinner while you stayed at home and looked after the house?

Couples often have pet names for each other. What pet names have you been given in the past?

I don't like unreliable men. How reliable are you?

How would you feel if you found out I was a traffic warden?

If I brought my Mum along on our blind date, how would you react?

I love horse-racing. If you were in my stable, why would you be my favourite horse?

If you were my father, how would you feel about my going out with a man like you?

I lived for 14 years in Barbados and really got to love the music. So, please, could you sing me a short calypso that tells me something about you?

Everybody says the Sixties were a really swinging time. So, I'd like you to tell me, what did you do then that was really swinging?

You're on a train without a corridor when six bad-tempered Hell's Angels get in and sit down next to you. What do you do?

You can tell a lot about a man from his feet. So – No.1, please describe No.2's feet. No.2, please describe No.3's feet. And No.3, please describe No.1's feet.

I like men to wear nice aftershave and smell good. So – No.1, tell me what No.2 smells of. No.2, tell me what No.3 smells of. And No.3, tell me what

No.1 smells of.

I'd love to be a film star. If you were a movie producer – judging me just on my voice – what sort of part would you cast me in?

If I rang you up in the middle of the night and told you there was an enormous spider in my bath, what would you do?

What is the one thing you would most like to change about yourself?

What dress style most turns you off in a woman?

Suppose we were out on our date together and we ran into one of your ex-girlfriends. What would you do?

Men seem to like my knobbly knees. What do women love about you?

I have to confess that I sometimes lie about my age. What do you lie about?

A few years ago, I was voted Barmaid of the Year. What national competition would you stand a chance of winning?

I go swimming twice a week, because it's free at the local baths. Of all the things you get free as a pensioner, what do you enjoy most?

Suppose I turned up for our date with purple hair and false eyelashes and looking like mutton dressed as lamb. How would you react?

I must admit I tend to talk rather a lot – as you may have noticed! How would you get a word in edgeways on our date?

I'm a cat lover. Is there anything feline about you, and, if so, what is it?

When you were a child, how did you react when

you were given a Christmas present that you really didn't like or want?

Which pantomime character do you most resemble – and why?

I never touch alcohol. How would this affect our date?

I'm a mean, aggressive and thoroughly nasty driver. What sort of passenger would you be in my car?

I'm a bit of an extrovert. If we were in a piano bar and I leapt up and began belting out a song, how would you react?

I'm studying to be a fashion designer. If I needed a male model to help me break into the fashion world, what sort of clothes would you be best at modelling?

Lying in bed one night, you hear a window smash downstairs and a burglar climbing in. What do you do?

You can tell a lot about people's characters from their faces. So, No.1, what shape is No.2's face and what is its most prominent feature? No.2, what shape is No.3's face and what is its most prominent feature? No.3, what shape is No.1's face and what is its most prominent feature?

Not long ago, I dyed my hair and it came out bright orange. Would you have gone out with me looking like that, and how would you have explained me to your friends?

Who is your ideal woman, and why would she be interested in you?

No.1, if you were casting No.2 in a film, what part or type of part would you give him – and why? No.2, if you were casting No.3 in a film, what part or type of part would you give him –

and why? No.3, if you were casting No.1 in a film, what part or type of part would you give him – and why?

I have a weak spot for big luxurious limo's. If you were a car, what type of car would you be?

Unlike most of my friends, I'm not an animal lover. In what way are you most different from your friends?

If you were a bookie, what odds would you give me that I would have a successful date with you – and why?

If you were staying the night at our house and saw me just as I was going to bed wearing a winceyette nightie and a hairnet and with my teeth in a glass, how would you react?

I used to do a lot of ballet, and I love it. Would you make a good ballet dancer – and, if so, why?

I like heroes. What sort of hero would you be?

I work in a man's world and I really enjoy it. What job would you like to do in a woman's world?

How intelligent are you?

When I'm bored, I often do extraordinary things. For instance, at a party recently, I put an egg between my knees and started clucking like a chicken. If you had been with me, how would you have reacted?

"

behave?

Who would you most like to see climbing down your chimney as Santa Claus - and what special present would you like him to bring you?

If you wanted to cook me a meal that would convince me you were a superb cook, what would it be?

I'm very interested in entertainment. Please do me an impression of your favourite show business personality.

I like girls to toe the line. What would you say if I asked you to iron my shirts?

If we were stuck in an igloo together for a week, how would you propose we kept warm?

Which character in a children's book do you most identify with - and why?

What, if anything, do you think makes you attractive to the opposite sex?

How would you feel about going out with a man considerably shorter than yourself?

At your office party, you're caught behind a filing cabinet with the office Romeo. How do you explain that away?

On a first date, I'm often so nervous I babble on non-stop and wave my arms about like Magnus Pyke. How would you calm me down and shut me up?

How would you prepare yourself for our date to make absolutely certain that I wasn't disappointed?

I run a singing telegram service. If I employed you, what sort of singing telegram would you specialize in?

What qualities do you most dislike in a man, and how would you correct them if you discovered I had any of them?

I like women to be feminine. What is the most feminine thing about you?

I'm rather unpunctual. If I kept you waiting on a street corner for half an hour, how would you amuse yourself until I showed up?

How would you get a man to do a job about the house without nagging him?

What would my mother least like about you?

I'm leaving on an overland trek to India tomorrow morning. Will you drop everything and come?

How would you behave if you were the mistress of a large country house?

What do you think of me so far?

I've got a very quick temper. How would you go about calming me down if I was really furious?

If all your friends disapproved of a man you were crazy about, would you drop him?

If you were writing an advertising slogan for yourself, what would it be?

Some girls are really put off by ravishingly handsome men. Could you cope?

How would you react if I criticized the way you dressed in public?

Do you fall in love often and, if so, how do you

One of my hobbies is collecting wine. If I were to add you to my collection, what sort of wine would you be?

If you could be someone famous for one day, who would it be – and why?

We're in a lift together and it breaks down. I get a violent attack of claustrophobia. What do you do?

I don't like women to use bad language. If you stub your toe or drop a teacup or something like that, what do you say?

My job is organizing parties for people. In what way would your job come in useful in our relationship?

Can you explain to me why women so rarely take men out to dinner?

I once spent three months as a cowboy on a farm in Australia. How would you fit in in the outback?

I rather like the outdoor type. Where are you most at home – a farmyard, a sportsfield or a beach?

If you discovered I was two-timing you with your best friend, who would you blame - her or me?

How often do you change your mind?

Suppose you invited me back to your flat and there was a power failure. In what way would that affect your plans for me?

Apart from your present one, what job would you most like to do in the whole world - and why?

I enjoy writing songs, and the song title that best describes me is "I'm Your Man". What song title best describes you?

I manage a health studio. What sort of exercise do you like taking most?

# BOYS, SO FAR

I play the guitar really badly - but I love it. What do you enjoy doing really badly?

Everybody resembles some animal or other. What animal are you most like?

One day I'm going to build myself a house. If you were building yourself a house, what special features would you like to include in it?

The last time you had a row with a man, what was it all about?

If we were in my local pub together, you might find that I was spending rather a lot of time chatting to my mates. How would you drag me away from them?

How would you react if a man you'd invited to dinner walked straight into the kitchen and insisted on cooking the meal himself?

What is your favourite drink, and how many do you need before you start becoming sentimental?

I love gardening. What would you look forward to most if I took you for a walk around my garden?

If we were out on a date, and you came back from the bar and found me kissing another girl, what would you do?

I like a woman to pay me a lot of compliments. So – judging me on my voice alone, describe me and tell me how much you love me.

I'm a perfectionist and little things annoy me. What little things annoy you?

What infuriates you most about men?

Which sports personality would you most like to go out with – and why?

I own a couple of nightclubs. If I offered you a job in one of them, what would you like to do?

If I have a fault, it's that I'm too generous. How would you stop me spending all my money on you?

If you suddenly acquired the power of hypnotism, who would you hypnotize and what would you get them to do?

I went to the Carnival in Brazil last year. If you were a Carnival Queen, what theme and type of costume would you choose?

I'm a typical Scotsman. If I turned up for our date wearing a kilt, would you be appalled, and where would you suggest we went for the evening?

I'm in the record business. If you had your own record label, what name would you give it that would reflect your personality?

I tend to look my worst first thing in the morning. When do you look your worst?

As part of an advertising campaign, I once spent a whole day walking up and down Oxford Street dressed as a giant hamburger – and got a lot of reaction. If you'd met me that day, what would you have said?

I have a phobia about water – particularly large waves. Would this be a problem in our relationship?

I believe you can always tell a woman's character by her clothes and the way she talks about another woman. Bearing that in mind – No.3, tell me what No.1 is wearing. No.1, tell me what No.2 is wearing. And No.2, tell me what No.3 is wearing.

How would you react if you found me in your stocking on Christmas morning?

If I have a fault – and, frankly, I don't think I have – it's that I tend to be rather big-headed. How would you cope with this?

If I were your true love, what would you like me to send you for Christmas? I want you to sing the answer. Now, are you ready…"On the first day of Christmas, my true love sent to me…"

I'm a chiropodist, but one thing I never talk about on a date is feet. What important part of your life would you prefer not to talk about?

What annoys you most about other people first thing in the morning?

I love eating. If you could be the dish of the day on my menu, what would you be – and why?

If I could go back in time, I would like to be an American gangster in the 1930s. What era would you like to go back to?

You are stopped at a traffic light when a car pulls up beside you with your ideal man behind the wheel. In the five seconds at your disposal, how would you attract his attention to arrange a date with him?

What colour best describes your temperament – and why?

I run a shop selling kitchen equipment. If I offered you some kitchenware as a present, what would you choose and what would you cook for me with it?

When buying trousers, I often have difficulty finding pairs with short enough legs. What physical problems do you have with clothes?

I invite you out on a hot date, but you don't want to come. What's your excuse? – and please make it convincing.

I love dancing. What's your favourite dance and how good are you at it?

My son lives in Australia and I go to visit him as often as I can. If I invited you to come with me, what part of the trip would you enjoy most?

I don't smoke and I don't drink very much. What don't you do?

Whenever I'm on a first date, the song "It's Now Or Never" runs though my head. What song do you think best sums up a first date?

I like women to be a challenge. In what way would you be one?

I like to think that I could be someone's ideal man. From what you've heard of me, whose ideal man do you think I'd be?

I play a lot of golf. If I invited you to accompany me round the course while I played, what would you enjoy most about the afternoon?

I'm very wary of being entrapped by a woman. How would you get round or break down my defences?

I'm very fond of fresh fruit. What fruit do you think you're most like – and why?

WELL, THOSE ARE THE QUESTIONS, AND, BELIEVE ME, WE GET ALL SORTS OF ANSWERS – FROM THE ROMANTIC . . .

"Suppose you invited me back to your flat and there was a power failure. In what way would that affect your plans for me?"

Wendy: "I definitely wouldn't do anything, because, you see, I might have arranged the power failure . . ."

. . . TO THE UNROMANTIC,

"I have to confess that I sometimes lie about my age. What do you lie about?"

Tony: "I lie about the house."

FROM THE BOASTFUL . . .

"I like women to be a challenge. In what way would you be one?"

Sharon: "Well, from what you said before about being a milkman, I think you'd need a lorra lorra bottle to go out with me."

. . . TO THE MODEST.

"If you were offered a free magazine subscription for life, which magazine would you choose?"

Joe: "The Beano."

# THE ANSWERS

## SOME OF THE ANSWERS ARE A BIT SMART . . .

"I don't like men with bad manners. Convince me you're a gentleman."

Tracy: "Well, I'd just say 'Thank you' afterwards, really."

## . . . WHILE SOME COULDN'T BE MORE INNOCENT.

"I'm in the record business. If you had your own record label, what name would you give it that would reflect your personality?"

Vanessa: "I'm afraid Richard Branson's already thought of it."

## SOME ARE EAGER . . .

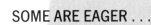

"You are stopped at a traffic light when a car pulls up beside you with your ideal man behind the wheel. In the five seconds at your disposal, how would you attract his attention to arrange a date with him?"

Claire: "I'd be driving a convertible, so I'd just take my top off so that you could get a better view."

## . . . WHILE OTHERS ARE COOOOOL.

"I invite you out for a hot date, but you don't want to come. What's your excuse? — and please make it convincing."

Judy: "I'd pick up the phone and I'd say 'Hullo, this is Judy. I'm sorry I'm not in right now, but if you leave your name and number after the tone, I'll get right back to you. Beeeeeeeeeeeeeeep!'"

SOME PEOPLE INDULGE IN EXTRAVAGANT FANTASY . . .

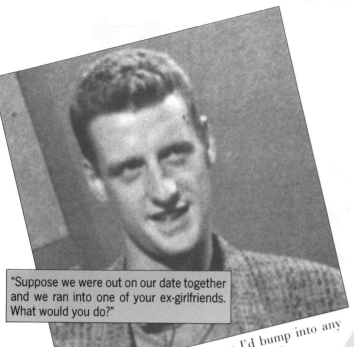

"Suppose we were out on our date together and we ran into one of your ex-girlfriends. What would you do?"

Jim: "There really is no chance I'd bump into any of my ex-girlfriends, because they're all in Hollywood, doing really well for themselves."

. . . WHILE SOME ARE BRUTALLY HONEST

"I play the guitar really badly, but I love it. What do you enjoy doing really badly?"

Tamsin: "Behaving. I love behaving badly."

SOME ARE JUST BRUTAL . . .

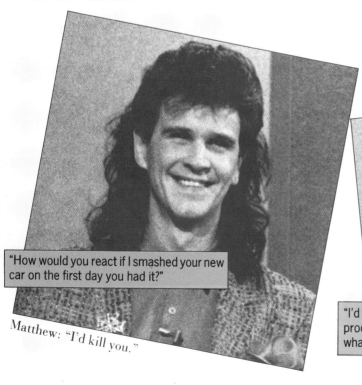

"How would you react if I smashed your new car on the first day you had it?"

Matthew: "I'd kill you."

. . . OTHERS ARE DOWNRIGHT RUDE.

"I'd love to be a film star. If you were a movie producer — judging me just on my voice — what sort of part would you cast me in?"

Vince: "As soon as I heard your voice, I knew you w destined for movies — silent movies."

THAT'S NOT NICE!

BUT THEY'RE NOT ALL COMEDIANS. WE CAN ALSO DO YOU SINGERS . . .

. . . IMPRESSIONISTS

. . . DANCERS

"On the first day of Christmas, my true love sent to me — "

Mandy: "A fella with a five year guarantee."

. . . . . AND EVEN POETS

Ian: "I'm hunkier than Robert Redford. I'm taller than Richard Gere. I'm fitter than Daley Thompson — You're extremely lucky I'm here."

Chet: "My name's Chet And I'm a good bet. I just can't wait To go on this Blind Date."

SAY WHAT YOU LIKE, THIS SHOW'S GOT MORE CULTURE THAN A PATH LAB. EAT YOUR HEART OUT, MELVYN BRAGG!

Here's a chance for you to see if you can pick your own ideal date. All you have to do is read the answers to the questions and decide which of the three possible partners you'd prefer to go on a blind date with. Then simply join up the dots to see who you've chosen.

## GIRLS, ASK AWAY!

**1.**      **ALL RIGHT, GUYS, HOW WOULD YOU FEEL IF THE GIRL YOU WERE GOING OUT WITH SAID SHE WAS GIVING YOU UP FOR A MAN WHO WAS MUCH SHORTER THAN YOU?**

Boy 1      Look honey, girls don't give me up. I give them up. OK?

Boy 2      I'd tread on him.

Boy 3      Impossible, no one's shorter than me. No, seriously, if that did happen, I guess I'd feel pretty small – even smaller.

**2.**      **IF YOU BECAME A GIRL FOR A DAY, WHAT'S THE FIRST THING YOU'D DO?**

Boy 1      Shave my chest.

Boy 2      I certainly wouldn't look in the mirror – God, I'd be ugly!

Boy 3      I'd come round to my apartment dolled up to the nines and throw myself at myself. Trouble is, with my luck, I'd probably be out.

**3.**      **WHAT ANIMAL WOULD YOU LIKE TO BE RE-INCARNATED AS?**

Boy 1      A ram. Or a stallion.

Boy 2      A newt.

Boy 3      A cockroach. I might get better breaks.

## BOYS, ASK AWAY!

**1.**      **IF I TOOK YOU HOME TO MEET MY PARENTS, WOULD YOU BEHAVE AS YOU NORMALLY DO, OR WOULD YOU PUT ON A BIT OF AN ACT?**

Girl 1      You bet I'd put on an act! I've got this far – I'm not letting you get away now.

Girl 2      Oh, my God. I loathe meeting boys' parents. The mother always hates me and never wants to see me again, and the father always likes me and *does* want to see me again. Alone.

Girl 3      I'm so glad to hear you have such strong family ties. I do so believe in the family. I'd be delighted to meet your parents. Does that answer your question?

**2.**      **WHICH PANTOMIME CHARACTER DO YOU MOST IDENTIFY WITH?**

Girl 1      An Ugly Sister – because I'm so lumpy.

Girl 2      The Sleeping Beauty. I'm lumpy too – but in the right places.

Girl 3      Snow White, because I'm icy cold and surround myself with dwarves.

**3.**      **SUPPOSE YOUR BEST FRIEND'S FELLA MADE A PASS AT YOU WHILE SHE WAS AWAY. HOW WOULD YOU REACT?**

Girl 1      Total shock. Nobody – not even Rugby players – makes a pass at me.

Girl 2      I wouldn't *dream* of going out with him. After all – why dream when you can do it for real?

Girl 3      That's a simple one. I don't have a best friend. And, if I did, I'd make sure she didn't have a 'fella', as you quaintly put it. She'd have to be totally loyal to me.

Boy 1

Boy 2

Boy 3

Girl 1

Girl 2

Girl 3

# WHO SAID WHAT?

HERE'S ANOTHER GAME FOR YOU TO PLAY. JUST
FROM THEIR APPEARANCE, SEE IF YOU CAN TELL
WHO SAID WHAT IN ANSWER TO THESE QUESTIONS.
(SOLUTION ON FINAL PAGE)

| Peter: Everybody resembles some animal or other. What animal are you most like? | | |
|---|---|---|
| | 1. | *A Chipmunk* |
| | 2. | *A Lion* |
| | 3. | *A Haggis* |

| David: I'm a typical Scotsman. If I turned up for our date wearing a kilt, where would you suggest we went for the evening? | | |
|---|---|---|
| | 1. | *Hang-gliding.* |
| | 2. | *You'll take the high road and I'll take the low road... and I'll look at the view.* |
| | 3. | *I'll take you for a romantic romp... through a field of thistles.* |

| Clare: I'm a cat lover. Is there anything feline about you, and, if so, what is it? | 1. *Like all cats, I'm always thrown out of the house when they go to bed, so I usually end up having a night on the tiles.* |
| --- | --- |
| | 2. *I think I'm purrfect... and eight out of ten cat owners prefer me.* |
| | 3. *I adore my tummy being tickled.* |

| Jan: Sing me a song that tells me something about you. | 1. *When I need you...* |
| --- | --- |
| | 2. *There once was an ugly duckling...* |
| | 3. *To all the girls I've loved before...* |

# THE MOMENT OF TRUTH

AFTER THE QUESTIONS AND ANSWERS COMES THE MOMENT OF DECISION FOR OUR PICKER – THE MOMENT TO DECIDE WHO TO TAKE ON THAT VERY SPECIAL BLIND DATE. IT'S NOT A CHOICE I'D EVER WANT TO HAVE TO MAKE, I CAN TELL YOU. BUT SPARE A THOUGHT, TOO, FOR THOSE THREE POOR SOULS ON THE OTHER SIDE OF THE SCREEN. WHAT'S GOING THROUGH THEIR MINDS?

*"I was a little bit horrified. He was really Jack the Lad and I just thought 'Maybe I don't want him to pick me'."*

*"I thought 'Crikey, just my luck. She's a Russian shot-putter with 5 o'clock shadow. Or somebody like Bette Midler. Or a female impersonator.'"*

*"Cilla had made a reference to this sort of bright shirt he was wearing, and I thought 'Oh, no, it's going to be a wally. He's going to be the sort of "Rock on, Tommy" type with this bright, flamboyant shirt and this really droll Northern accent.'"*

WELL, TOUGH LUCK, I'M AFRAID, BECAUSE THERE'S NOTHING THEY CAN DO ABOUT IT NOW, IS THERE? IT'S THE PICKER'S DECISION, AND THE PICKER'S DECISION ALONE – WHICH DOESN'T MAKE IT ANY MORE SENSIBLE WHEN IT COMES.

*" Will you choose No. 1, who's really a home-loving girl, so, if you've got a stately home, she'll just love it. Or No. 2, a girl who wants to live life in the fast lane – of the cycle path. Or will it be No. 3, who is lithe, lean, luscious – and lying. The decision ... is yours."*

*"At the time I was sitting on the chair and you really are nervous, and of course Cilla is asking you if you've made your mind up, so you really are under a lot of pressure. But the thing that sticks in my mind is when Dawn did her trumpet solo, so I thought she'd be good for a day out."*

*"I decided to pick Debbie, because the very first question I asked she answered perfectly – she talked about foot and mouth disease."*

AND SO THE DECISION IS MADE. THE TWO UNLUCKY CONTESTANTS STEP FORWARD FOR A QUICK HULLO AND GOODBYE AND THE MOMENT OF TRUTH ARRIVES. HOW'S THE LUCKY WINNER FEELING NOW? I WONDER...

*"I edged towards the screen and I thought 'Ye Gods, George, what have you gone and let yourself in for now?' I wondered what old bat was on the other side."*

*"One thing did worry me – she was a policewoman. I thought that she was going to be fairly strict. I thought that I was going to regret this."*

THE ONE THAT GOT AWAY.....

# HERE IS YOUR BLIND DATE!

*"The thing that really stood out was his mouth. It was – rotten to say – it wasn't that big, but it was...well, you know, it was big actually, yeah."*

*"When I saw Debbie, my heart just sunk – it did, really. She was the best looking girl I've ever seen, even on the whole BLIND DATE series. I've watched them all, and for just physical appearance she was ten out of ten."*

*"When they pulled the screen back and the girl stood there in a bright yellow dress, and Cilla was stood next to her in a big purple leather suit, it was one of the most revolting combinations I've seen in a long time."*

*"When the slide went back on the screen, I was hoping that I would see Clint Eastwood. All I found was Clyde, Clint Eastwood's orang-utan."*

*"There was this 4'3" young lady who wasn't my type at all straight away. I mean, that's before I knew what sort of girl she was. When I got to know what sort of girl she was – it was worse."*

*"I thought he looked like a Christmas tree. You know – white socks, painted shoes. I suspect he's got tattoos everywhere."*

*"When I first saw Rorie, well, there's tall men and tall men. I just all went to pieces. I couldn't really kiss his navel."*

*"She looked fairly startled and I decided to grab her as quickly as I could... The other point that sticks in my mind is that she had very large feet. I recall that at the time I thought that she was possibly a good swimmer."*

*"I looked at her and she looked at me and I thought 'Yes, she's nice. Very nice blonde hair. It might be dyed – I don't know.'"*

*"She'd had her hair done for the show, and it was like this large lion's mane around her head. And the clothes she was wearing at the time weren't that complementary, so she looked like a dandelion in a tent really."*

*"Right from the beginning, he seemed to get the impression that I hated him. Well, he wasn't far wrong."*

*"I'm sure I heard her grunt or groan when she saw me, so the reactions were virtually the same. Neither of us was over-impressed with the other."*

*"I just grabbed hold of her and lifted her in the air. There's 500 people watching in a live audience, and I just grabbed her as if there was no one there."*

*"It was such a relief to have somebody who I wouldn't be ashamed to walk into my local wine bar with."*

*"She wasn't at all like what I expected she would be. She looked like she had a lot more intelligence than the sort of woman I would expect to go on BLIND DATE."*

Spot the poser(s).

Two who didn't get picked console each other.

"Please – I said no press!"

WELL, AFTER THE SHOW, WE ALL GO UPSTAIRS TO
GETS TO MEET EVERYONE ELSE WHO THEY'VE BEEN
I'D REALLY LIKE TO DO

The Hon. Gervase Ffanshawe and Miss Venetia Maltravers (also known as Andrew and Judy).

And now a number from the Blind Date Be-Bop Balladeers.

Giles tells Rekha one of his jokes.

Richard is not amused.

Michael can't believe what he's hearing.

# SHOW IS OVER

A rose between two thorns.

One of these people, believe it or not, is a psychiatrist.

What's this? Marriage guidance?

HAVE A SARNIE AND A GLASS OF WINE, AND EVERYONE
KEPT APART FROM ALL DAY. THERE ARE TIMES I THINK
THE SHOW UP HERE . . .

When they start doing the conga, you know it's time to go home.

"Will all passengers for flight IB609 please go to departure gate 7?"

Nony tells everyone where to go.

A goodnight kiss from Mike.

"Say goodnight, Karen. Goodnight!"

# MAP OF ALL THE DATES

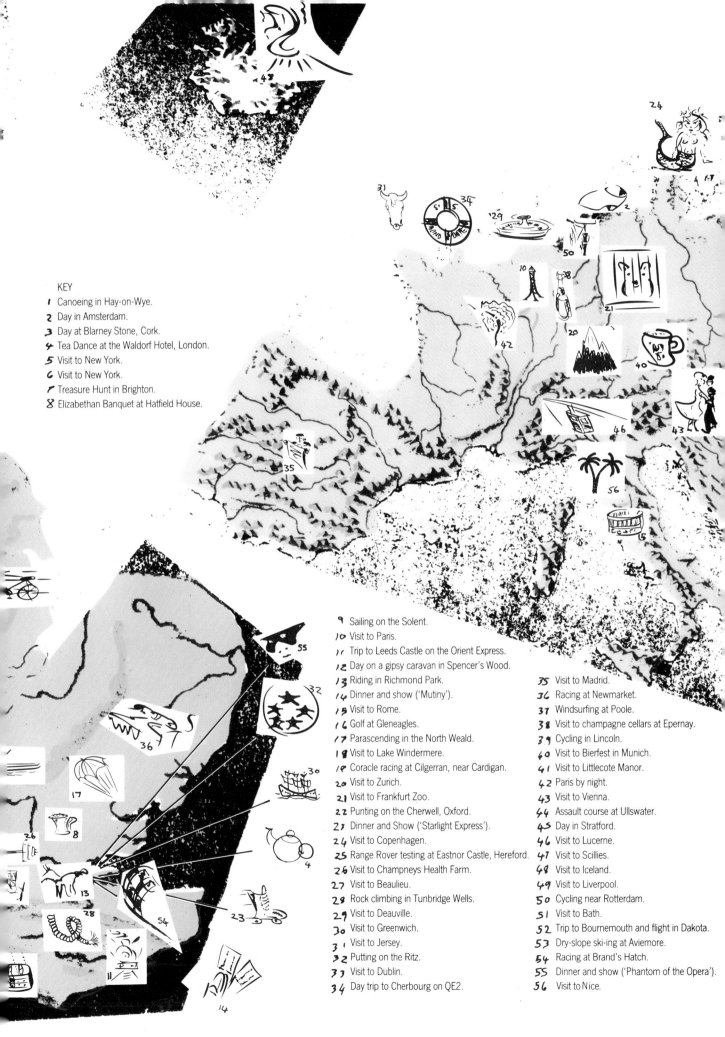

KEY
1 Canoeing in Hay-on-Wye.
2 Day in Amsterdam.
3 Day at Blarney Stone, Cork.
4 Tea Dance at the Waldorf Hotel, London.
5 Visit to New York.
6 Visit to New York.
7 Treasure Hunt in Brighton.
8 Elizabethan Banquet at Hatfield House.

9 Sailing on the Solent.
10 Visit to Paris.
11 Trip to Leeds Castle on the Orient Express.
12 Day on a gipsy caravan in Spencer's Wood.
13 Riding in Richmond Park.
14 Dinner and show ('Mutiny').
15 Visit to Rome.
16 Golf at Gleneagles.
17 Parascending in the North Weald.
18 Visit to Lake Windermere.
19 Coracle racing at Cilgerran, near Cardigan.
20 Visit to Zurich.
21 Visit to Frankfurt Zoo.
22 Punting on the Cherwell, Oxford.
23 Dinner and Show ('Starlight Express').
24 Visit to Copenhagen.
25 Range Rover testing at Eastnor Castle, Hereford.
26 Visit to Champneys Health Farm.
27 Visit to Beaulieu.
28 Rock climbing in Tunbridge Wells.
29 Visit to Deauville.
30 Visit to Greenwich.
31 Visit to Jersey.
32 Putting on the Ritz.
33 Visit to Dublin.
34 Day trip to Cherbourg on QE2.

35 Visit to Madrid.
36 Racing at Newmarket.
37 Windsurfing at Poole.
38 Visit to champagne cellars at Epernay.
39 Cycling in Lincoln.
40 Visit to Bierfest in Munich.
41 Visit to Littlecote Manor.
42 Paris by night.
43 Visit to Vienna.
44 Assault course at Ullswater.
45 Day in Stratford.
46 Visit to Lucerne.
47 Visit to Scillies.
48 Visit to Iceland.
49 Visit to Liverpool.
50 Cycling near Rotterdam.
51 Visit to Bath.
52 Trip to Bournemouth and flight in Dakota.
53 Dry-slope ski-ing at Aviemore.
54 Racing at Brand's Hatch.
55 Dinner and show ('Phantom of the Opera').
56 Visit to Nice.

## ROMANCE GOT OFF TO A BAD START WHEN CLARE AND JON WENT TO VIENNA.

## THAT EVENING, THE CONVERSATION TURNED TO MARRIAGE.

## IN FACT, IT'S NOT UNUSUAL FOR THE HAPPY COUPLE TO HAVE SECOND THOUGHTS AS SOON AS THEY SET EYES ON EACH OTHER THE NEXT DAY . . .

"He was wearing plastic shades to cover his baggy eyes from the night before, because he'd been out on the drink, celebrating his birthday. He was smelling of drink, like a brewery, breathing all over me."

"He was three minutes late – as he reminded me, 'cos I couldn't have cared less if he'd been two hours late, quite honestly. I mean, I really wasn't that bothered."

"We arrived early in the morning at Gatwick for the departure. In fact, Martine had arrived earlier. I suppose she was just desperate to be with me."

"I met her in the bar, and I realized then when I saw her that it wasn't a dream and she did actually look like that."

## ONE OR TWO ARE STRANGELY SILENT.

"She was bouncing along, really quite content and happy, and I saw she had a spot on her nose. I said 'I've got to let you know you've got a nice horrible little spot there. You must be really concerned about it. So I thought I'd just let you know, just to put you on edge and make you feel uncomfortable with me.' "

"I bought her a dozen red roses. I've never bought flowers for a girl before. I mentioned I was going on Blind Date, so I got a couple of quid off."

"He started talking about test-tube babies and artificial insemination and I wondered what on earth I had let myself in for."

"With it being Sarah's 21st birthday, I thought 'I'll buy her a lovely box of chocolates.' So I presented these to her when I met her, and they were Terry's All Gold, and the first thing she said was 'Oh, I hate plain chocolates, but it'll be a great present for my mother.' So I thought 'That's going to be a great start, isn't it?' "

"She's got a nice quiet personality – quiet to the extent that she fell asleep on numerous occasions."

"She told me my jokes were corny, so I didn't tell any more, so that was the end of the conversation. So I put my coat over my head and went to sleep."

## ONE THING THEY ALL SEEM TO HAVE SOMETHING TO SAY ABOUT IS THEIR PARTNER'S CLOTHES.

"I saw this chap standing by the limousine dressed as Biggles and I thought 'Oh, my God – that's my Blind Date.' "

"He chewed gum all day, probably because it was the only exercise his jaw got – because he didn't actually speak very much, so it was probably to keep his jaws going."

"We had a lovely meal – champagne and king prawns and lobster. There wasn't much conversation, but the lobster was quite friendly."

"Paul started to read his newspaper, and there wasn't really a lot to read on the plane other then the sick bag, so I ended up looking out of the window."

"I thought she would strike up conversation or something, but she just snored away in the background – sort of mingled in with the engines of the plane."

"The actual dress she wore on the particular night . . . she said it cost £150. I think I could probably have made one for at least half the cost.

"She looked stunning. Wearing a lovely black dress. How she got into it I will never know. She must have been poured in."

"I realized that no expense had been spared for the outfit, because she asked me if there was anywhere I could put her 90 pence earrings."

"It was slightly embarrassing at times to find other couples going round in very high class fashion and he had a Scoobidoo tee-shirt on."

## AND A FEW GO RIGHT TO THE OTHER EXTREME.

"She talks too much. She was vaccinated with a gramophone needle."

"I realized he didn't have much of a brain and he was very posey and mouthy, so I put my Walkman on, preferring that instead."

"She's just a total motormouth. You definitely need a good pair of ears to listen to it."

"She was giving me G.B.H. of the ear at 39,000 feet at the speed of sound."

"I got the odd word in now and again, but as a rule I was just told to shut up and listen."

"She couldn't eat dairy products, because she told me it depressed her and stopped her talking. So there I was all day, trying to push these dairy products down her throat."

# THE DAY OF THE DATE

"I could not get over the way she just kept pouring smoked salmon down her cakehole. It was like seeing Jaws on dry dock."

"I had some sausages and sauerkraut and Dawn had about three chickens. She can certainly put it away."

"I ordered stuffed peppers for two simply because that was the only thing I could pronounce on the menu."

"After all the meals she ate, it was incredible how the helicopter got off the ground."

"They brought this fantastic trolley and it was just laden with every possible dessert you could imagine, all beautifully displayed. And this waiter went through it all in English and explained what they'd done with this and what they'd done with that. And after he'd spent about ten minutes doing this, Clare just said 'Can I have some vanilla ice cream, please?' "

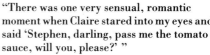

"There was one very sensual, romantic moment when Claire stared into my eyes and said 'Stephen, darling, pass me the tomato sauce, will you, please?' "

## . . . UNLESS IT'S HAVING A DRINK TOGETHER.

"He was drinking lager, you know. He thought 'Great – free beer'. And he was knocking them back, glass after glass after glass. And he didn't realize that it was non-alcoholic lager."

"I wasn't too sure whether it was meant to be blind drunk or Blind Date that day."

"We sort of went halfie-halfies on the drinks and, because I only had 4 and she had 32, it was a little bit unfair, I think."

"Helen likes the occasional drink. The reason why I say 'occasional' was she spilt most of it. All over my trousers."

"When it came to ordering the wine, she gave me permission to look at the wine list."

"It's not that Giles drank a lot. It just seemed that periodically throughout the day he just said he'd like a drink fairly often."

"He asked me what wine I liked, and I said that I liked German wine. So he ordered a bottle of French."

## BUT, BY THE END OF THE DAY, THEY'RE NEARLY ALWAYS EXHAUSTED . . .

"After kissing the Blarney Stone, theoretically you should have the gift of the gab, but he actually fell asleep on the way back."

"The tiredness had caught up with both of us, and she was nodding off in the passenger seat, and she started to dribble, dribble down the side of her chin."

"I went to sleep, 'cos I was that tired. I don't know whether he did. I think he went to sleep, but I wouldn't swear to it – 'cos I couldn't see him, 'cos I was asleep."

"I woke up and we were just coming to the airport, and I said 'I hope I wasn't snoring.' And she said – she didn't say anything. She was asleep herself."

"I'll always remember Stratford with Debbie..."

"She had what I call natural beauty. She was a beautiful person, without being too Californian, she really was. She was really beautiful."

"She had such a lovely mouth. It was a nice memory for me."

"When she said 'Well, that's dead good', it really sort of did something inside me. You get a frothy feeling – I can't explain – it's like butterflies. No, when she said 'Dead good'... it made me melt."

# "WHEREFORE ART THOU, DEBBIE?"

"We didn't have one argument. There wasn't one moment on the whole day that I felt 'My God, what am I doing?'"

"I think she was very well brought up. I find that a lot of girls are into themselves and into their make-up and their image, whereas she was more her own person."

"The body language was right as well."

"Why did I say I could ride? I was scared to death... but I just held my breath and thought 'Well, I don't care. I'm with Debbie, and if anything happens to me, she'll look after me.'"

"I like sporty women – you know, a girl who looks after her body. She had a really fantastic body – I know, because she wore a bikini in the swimming pool."

"She's the sort of girl I'd like to have gone to school with, and we'd have gone out together – you know how that happens sometimes. It's sort of magical: you go out for ever, and that's the end..."

# DEAR CILLA . . .

Dear Gina,
Quite a lucky day we all in all. The first horse we backed was Dallas, a waitress gave us the tip, and to top it all, it came first. Amanda was screaming in the stands. We then went up to the winners' enclosure to meet the owner of the horse. It was Walter Matthau. And, of course, she Amanda loved that. She got his autograph and everything — the only thing that spoilt it really is that his horse that we'd just won £70 on trod on her toe, and she was screaming again!
See you next week, Paul

Cilla Black
Blind Date
LWT
LOND___

Dear Cilla,
Everywhere we go in Rome, Alyson keeps going up to all those foreigners and kissing them! It's so funny. Every time I turn round, she's kissing another Italian!
We invited this other couple to join us at lunch, a guy and his mother, who was a really lovable person. We spent about ½ an hour with them. When they left, Alyson gave him a nice kiss, and for once I did manage to kiss a lady — a 92 year old lady, but she was lovely!
Arriverderci Cilla — Gary

CILLA BLACK
BLIND DATE
LWT
LONDON
ENGLAND

Hi, Cilla!
What a great day we've had in champagne. I forgot my passport, so when we got over to France, Mary went straight through customs, and I was standing there looking at this mademoiselle and she was going "Passport! Passport!" so I said "No passport! No passport!" and she was asking for identification, so I showed her my Chester to Euston rail ticket and she wasn't impressed, so then I showed her my Access card and she went "That'll do nicely! That'll do nicely!" — and I was in!
Tara for now from Mary and me Philip

Cilla Black
Blind D___
L.W.___
LON___
AN___TERRE

Dear Cilla,
This part of Wales we've been in is lovely, but I never really got the hang of the coracle racing. Hugh's a very nice person, but because he's been so nice all the while, he's tended to bug me. I'm into women's lib more than a lot of girls are, and I like opening doors myself and sitting down myself. I must say, though, after Hugh being such a gentleman all day, I was rather shocked when he stuffed an ice cream in my face. Anyway, love from us both, Jane.

CILLA BLACK

BLIND DATE

L·W·T

LONDON

Dear Cilla,
Karen and I have had a wonderful day here in Deauville. One thing happened in the Casino that made me laugh. All day I'd been admiring how nice Karen's long, shiny, manicured nails were, but then she put her hand on the roulette wheel and this nail just sort of flew off into the distance and was gone forever, and underneath there was this white stubby chewed nail! I don't think she was too pleased!
Bye for now.
Martin.

Cilla Black

Blind Date.

L W T

LONDON

ENGLAND

# CHERYL AND GEOFF IN 'HAVE AN ICE DAY'

## THE MOMENT CHERYL AND GEOFF ARRIVED IN ICELAND THE CHASE BEGAN...

## ALL AFTERNOON, GEOFF KEPT UP THE PURSUIT...

AND THEY FOUGHT HAPPILY EVER AFTER.

# SPILLING THE BEANS . . . .

AFTER THE DATE, THE RECKONING. A DAY OR TWO AFTER THE COUPLE HAVE GONE OUT, WE ASK THEM TO COME BACK TO TELL US ALL ABOUT EACH OTHER (SEPARATELY, OF COURSE!) IN FRONT OF A CAMERA. IT'S NOT AS DAUNTING AS IT SOUNDS, AS BILL, ONE OF THE LADS WHO GOT PICKED, TOLD US LATER . . .

**Telling the tale**

**The story unfolds**

*I had a word with the tall guy with the curly hair. We went down to the canteen and we had a coffee, and then he started asking me about the day and how we got on. He wangles things out of you. He roots around and wheedles for stories. He's got a list of questions, obviously, that get the most out of you, and then he digs a bit deeper and, if that's a good story – "Write it down, we'll mention it." I thought it would be something like, "Tell us something bad about her" or "Make it entertaining" – but the truth came out in the end – there was no lies to be told. And then he tells you what to do when you're on camera, which is helpful. I was confident, I wasn't at all nervous then. I didn't like looking at myself on the telly – there's a telly over there, and I thought "What a mess! How can you appear on television with a face like that? This is family viewing".*

*I was in there about 20 minutes - it flew by. We went through everything, and the bits that I'd messed up or sort of waffled on too much, we went over again. You told about the day and, if you went off the subject or whatever, they asked you a question to get more of it on the line of what you were after. You just wanted to eliminate all the waffle bits and get down to the nitty-gritty.*

**Waiting in the wings**

**Last minute chat**

*When I saw the interviews cut together in the studio, it surprised me. I was more surprised at my own voice – it sounded so thick. I think I've just got a normal plain accent, but when I came on the television, I sounded absolutely broad Blackburn . . . I was surprised how many nice things I said about her. I was convinced I'd been really nasty. I'd gone home and thought "Oh, no – I shouldn't have said that! Oh, God, what did I say that for? I bet she's not said it about me." And when I came back, in fact she'd said worse things about me than I'd said about her!*

**In the hot seat**

**"Quiet, please!"**

**"Action!"**

# . . OR NOT, AS THE CASE MAY BE.

UNFORTUNATELY, NOT EVERYONE IS AS OPEN AS OUR BILL THERE. SOME OF THEM ARE A BIT HESITANT ABOUT TELLING THE TRUTH, THE WHOLE TRUTH AND NOTHING BUT THE TRUTH . . .

**"He was an absolute wally, but I'm not going to say that. After all, the poor boy has got a mother."**

MAYBE HIS MOTHER WOULD AGREE WITH YOU!

MIND YOU, EVEN WHEN THEY SPEAK IN CODE, AS A LOT OF THEM DO, IT'S NOT THAT HARD TO WORK OUT WHAT THEY REALLY MEAN . . .

| WHAT THEY SAY | WHAT THEY MEAN |
|---|---|
| *"He's a very romantic guy."* | *"He's a wimp."* |
| *"He's not at all romantic."* | *"He's a brute."* |
| *"She was a good listener."* | *"She was incapable of coherent speech."* |
| *"She could have made a bit more effort in her appearance."* | *"She looked like a sack of football boots."* |
| *"He was a gentleman all day."* | *"He was terrified I was going to say something nasty about him now."* |
| *"Nice personality."* | *"Shame about the face."* |
| *"I prefer girls a bit rounder."* | *"I've seen telegraph poles with better figures."* |
| *"I'm really glad I picked her."* | *"I saw the other two."* |

AND HERE ARE A COUPLE OF THINGS THEY *DID* SAY – BUT WISHED THEY HADN'T – THAT *WE* DECIDED WE COULDN'T USE

WHOOPS

**"There's only one habit that I could pick fault with – she smoked. But she did agree on the day not to smoke so much. Oh, hell, her dad doesn't realize she smokes, I've just realized!"**

**"My father doesn't mind who I go out with. My mother I really don't take a great deal of notice of. God, I can't say that – she'll kill me!"**

WELL, SPEAKING AS A MOTHER MESELF – I WOULDN'T BLAME HER!

**"WELL, WHAT DID YOU SAY ABOUT ME?"**

**"THANKS FOR NOT BLOWING THE GAFF."**

# THE THINGS

MIND YOU, SOMETIMES YOU DO WONDER IF THE TWO OF THEM ACTUALLY WENT ON THE SAME DATE TOGETHER...

HIM: "The journey took two and a half hours and we just chatted."

HER: "The flight was two and a half hours, I think. And we both fell asleep."

HIM: "It was an intimate meal."

HER: "He never stopped burping all through the meal."

HER: "He's a very careful person with his money. And I'm just the opposite. I'll spend every ha'penny – which I did."

HIM: "I think she is a very careful person with money. I would say she's a thrifty person."

HIM: "I've got rhythm. I mean, I can dance at a disco' – that sort of thing."

HER: "He had absolutely no sense of rhythm."

HER: "The pilot gave us a complimentary bottle of champagne. Desa very kindly gave it to me before we got off the plane at the other end."

HIM: "I didn't want to part with it, but she persuaded me with a crisp £10 note."

HIM: "This horse – I'm not joking – I mean, it was like something out of a cartoon film. I mean, it had a slumped back and a big fat belly, and its legs were buckling and it had the ugliest face."

HER: "He was great – better looking than Matthew."

HIM: "We went to the Old Curiosity Shop, as in Dickens, and I tried to impress her with my knowledge of art and literature ... which I don't have any. She saw through me straight away and knew that I was bluffing."

HER: "He kept quoting lines from *Oliver* and *Nicholas Nickleby*, so he was quite well-read, although he claimed ignorance. I think that was to make me feel knowledgeable and intelligent, and not to make me feel small."

HER:
He had a lot of stories to tell about his time in the army. Every little thing that we did had some connection with when he was in the army.
HIM:
We didn't speak about the army. I don't like speaking about it.

HER:
"It was quite entertaining on the beach, because he spent all the time comparing the topless ladies with Samantha Fox."
HIM:
"There were some other girls on the beach, but I didn't really need to look at them, 'cos I was with Karen, and that was enough for me."

# THEY SAY

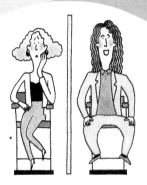

HER:
"He's a nice guy. A bit immature for his age. Probably not really lively enough to keep up with me."

HIM:
"I do think I'm slightly more mature than she is. And she could have been a bit livelier."

BUT, AT THE END, WE ALWAYS ASK THEM TO SUM UP THE DAY . . .

"A half-day would definitely have been better."

"She said that she didn't have a regular boyfriend. I suppose, to be quite honest, if she gives off the vibes to everybody else that she gave to me, it was really hardly surprising."

"We had nothing in common – only perhaps our hair-spray."

"She's rather more the wine bar and beanbag type of person, and I rather stick to pubs, really."

"We had a great day out, but just one peck on the cheek is not good enough. A man like me needs more than one peck."

"I got on quite well with him when we were apart."

"The very fact that she was prepared to spend the day with me was an endearing quality and one that I would recommend in other women."

"If I'd have been on a Blind Date in real life with him, I don't think I'd have stayed longer than ten minutes."

"The whole thing was like a big dream, and I was actually going to say I was glad to share it with her, but she'd probably slap me."

"I think a good date for me and Paul to go on would be a trip to the local morgue."

"I didn't fancy him and he didn't fancy me. He fancied himself, and I fancied myself."

"He did look to be sort of 'I'm it, I'm God's gift'. And he thought he was. And he probably is on Merseyside."

"My father would have liked her good sense of humour and my mother would have said that, if I was happy with her, she would be happy. I'm going to throw up . . ."

"I think she must have thought I was a conceited, arrogant, half-demented drunkard. I think she basically summed me up quite well, actually."

"On the way back in the helicopter, we were looking at all the sights out of the window, and I turned and was looking at Sallie, and she was looking out of the window, and I just wished she was looking at me to end the day."

## MIKE AND SARAH

MIKE:
*"I think you're a lovely girl and don't forget me in a hurry."*

SARAH:
*"Basically he's just a fantastic guy and the woman that one day pins him down is going to be very lucky."*

◀

## GARY AND HELEN

GARY:
*"She was good company and everything we did was just good fun and we had a good laugh and, um yeah, Mr Warren, what a nice daughter you've got!"*

HELEN:
*"Gary was great fun. He never stopped talking and was ever so easy going. I felt like I'd known him for years. Very polite, wonderful manners, it really would be very difficult to fault him."*

▶

## DAVID AND LIZ

LIZ:
*"He has these really nice blue eyes that just look so calm and nice and gentle, which he was – he was very gentle all day."*

DAVID:
*"She's the sort of girl who would have a lot of fellas chasing after her, a lot of suitors – and if there were a line of suitors, I would gladly be in that line, and I'd probably cheat to get to the top of it as well."*

◀

## JANET AND NICK

NICK:
*"I think we're probably going to get married, mmmmmm, Janet and I got on that well! No, seriously..."*

JANET:
*"I thought, well, haven't I done well! He was very smartly dressed and quite trendy in his appearance – and I loved his eyes. That's what caught my attention first, you know, when I looked at him first. I thought, what lovely eyes that guy's got."*

▶

## ALISTAIR AND SUE

**SUE:**
"He was wearing a suit and a thin red tie for the show, if you remember, and I think thin ties are very dodgy on men, very. Very dodgy, because the sort of men who wear thin red ties are usually smooth, very like 'Okay, chicks, I'm here — it's happening' when in actual fact they're not there and nothing's happening."

**ALISTAIR:**
"A suitable lady for me Sue is not. I'm sure she'll find maybe what she's looking for, but I wouldn't be it. I'd quite like to take her out if I lived next door to her, she's the sort of girl you could go to the pub with and maybe spend the evening or maybe you could have a game of darts with."

## WENDY AND MATTHEW

**WENDY:**
"Basically I'd rather have gone out with the horse and had a day on my own."
"The bad things about him that I don't like about him? His hair, his mannerisms, smelling of drink, the clothes he wears, the jewellery, his shoes, his attitude — I think he's quite ignorant, just a disco Joe type."

**MATTHEW:**
"Bad points — very pushy, talks without listening or doesn't care what anybody else says, just carries on in her own way — very hypo as well."
"She was small and, well, she was slim and small which was an advantage and that was about her only advantage really."

## MANDY AND SIMON

**SIMON:**
"She had this really nice tiny face that I found quite cute and dinky, that sort of appealed to me. Just the smallness of her face really... that you could put your hands around and strangle it."

**MANDY:**
"The lunch was very, very good; it was just a pity I had to share it with him."

## ALISON AND DESA

**ALISON:**
"I was expecting my answer to Prince Andrew and all I got was this hairy DJ from Birkenhead."

**DESA:**
"There were a few things that annoyed me about Alison. Um, one is that she had this high-pitched whining voice which on the odd occasions when she did speak, really drove me mad."

# Golden Oldies
## Edith and George in Gay Paree

Edith picks a card and reads out
'Pot-holing! Look at poor George's face!'

When the car breaks down, guess
who has to push the damn thing!

The Duke and Duchess of Paris!

Edith's first taste of champagne.
She's hooked on it now!

Two of the dancers at the
Moulin Rouge!

'Thanks Edith, for choosing me
as your date.'

Evie and Gerald 'Putting on the Ritz'

'Two Ritz Crackers'

We feel like Royalty—
look like it too!

Lunch.
Gerald makes a piggy of himself!

'Wonderful Day'

Evie asks to have one of the cast
gift wrapped—Gerald gets called an
old smoothie!

Evie agrees to visit Gerald—provided
there are chains on the doors!

# SOFA TALK

Fig A. line 1

'Our Blind Date was a great
success.'

HOW DO YOU THINK THIS COUPLE GOT ON?

AND SO TO ONE OF MY FAVOURITE BITS OF THE SHOW, WHEN OUR COUPLES COME BACK AND SIT ON THE SOFA AND WATCH WHAT THEY'VE SAID ABOUT EACH OTHER IN THAT LITTLE BOX AT THE BOTTOM OF THE SCREEN. ACTUALLY, BEFORE WE EVEN LISTEN TO THE EDITED INTERVIEWS. IT'S USUALLY POSSIBLE TO TELL HOW THEY GOT ON, JUST FROM THE WAY THEY SIT, AND HOW THEY USE THE CUSHIONS ON THE SOFA ...

YES, YOU'RE RIGHT – THEY GOT ON FAMOUSLY. THAT'S MANDY AND RICHARD, WHO WENT TO NICE FOR THEIR BLIND DATE. AND RICHARD TOLD US IN HIS INTERVIEW THAT MANDY PUT EVERYTHING THAT WASN'T NAILED DOWN ON THE AEROPLANE INTO A SICK BAG. I ASKED HER WHY AND SHE SAID:

"I just wanted to remember it, Cilla, because it was such a nice day, and I just took the mineral water and things like that . . ."

TO WHICH RICHARD ADDED:

". . . and the salt, pepper, mustard, knives, forks, spoons, serviettes, box of chocolates – didn't she do well?

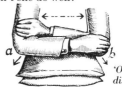

'Our Blind Date was a disaster.'

IN FACT, MOST OF OUR COUPLES ARE PRETTY FRANK WHEN THEY COME AND SIT ON THE SOFA. WHEN CLARE SAID TO JON:

"Why have you got grey hair as well?",

HE SNAPPED BACK:

"Two days in Vienna with you, dear!"

AND I'LL NEVER FORGET THE TIME I PLEADED WITH ONE LAD TO SAY SOMETHING NICE ABOUT HIS DATE. FINALLY HE CAME UP WITH:

"Um . . . er . . . um . . . she's a girl!"

'This person next to me is embarrassing.'

NOT EVERYONE'S LIKE THAT, OF COURSE. GEOFF AND CHERYL, WHO WENT TO ICELAND, WERE STILL VERY ROMANTIC, THOUGH. NEEDLESS TO SAY, THEY STILL COULDN'T AGREE ABOUT THE DETAILS:

Cheryl: "He keeps phoning me up unreasonable hours' in the morning, saying 'I love yer, I really love yer, wiv all these girls, yer know, and I'm a DJ and all this, and it's you I could really fall in love with'."

Geoff: "Just tell the truth. Half past one the other morning, she phoned me up . . . 'I've just come in from a nightclub, and I thought I'd phone to see if you still love me'."

BUT WHAT OF THE FUTURE? – THAT'S WHAT EVERYONE WANTS TO KNOW. DO OUR COUPLES STICK TOGETHER? WELL, MOST OF THEM AREN'T VERY HOPEFUL:

"I'd probably see him again if I bumped into him."

"I don't think I'm going to see him again. I might say Hello to him if I passed him in the street."

"I'd see him as a friend, but, um, no, I won't marry him. definitely not. No – he can take the kids back – I don't want them either."

AND LOOK WHAT OUR EDITH, THE MERRY WIDOW SAID, WHEN SHE WAS ASKED IF ANYTHING WAS LIKELY TO COME OUT OF HER TRIP TO PARIS WITH GEORGE:

"No . . . we're old and it was just a bit of fun. I don't want any more of it. I don't want to wash any more underpants."

AND WHEN I ASKED HER ON THE SOFA IF SHE HADN'T CHANGED HER MIND, SHE SAID:

"I'm too old for romance, too old. I'd rather have a good dinner."

'Help! I want my teddy bear!'

AND THE YOUNG ONES ARE USUALLY JUST AS UNROMANTIC. HERE'S DEBBIE AND ORHAN:

"We'll send each other birthday cards and Christmas cards . . ."

"Or letter bombs, yeah . . ."

AND GARY:

"Any time I'm in Wales, I'll pop down for a little drink."

"How often are you in Wales, then?"

"Ha ha ha – I've never been!"

AND THE MOST CUTTING REPLY OF ALL:

"The only way I'd talk to this man again is through a medium."

KIND OF "DO YOU WANT TO COME OUT TONIGHT? – ONE KNOCK FOR YES, TWO KNOCKS FOR NO"!

'How dare you say we didn't get on?'

BUT IT ISN'T HOPELESS. CHERYL SAID SHE AND GEOFF WERE "DEFINITELY" GOING TO SEE EACH OTHER AGAIN, AND, ALTHOUGH WE DON'T GET MANY LONG-TERM ROMANCES. THINGS DO TEND TO HAPPEN TO PEOPLE WHO'VE BEEN ON THE SHOW FOR MONTHS AFTERWARDS. TURN OVER AND FIND OUT MORE . . .

## DIRTY DEN SIGNING SHOCK

The ratings-mad world of TV was still reeling tonight after Beeb superstar Leslie Grantham met his match at a crazy autograph session at a trade Sports Exhibition in London.

While *East Enders* heart-throb Leslie scribbled away for adoring fans, his wife chatted to sports shop owner Gary of North Wales, who appeared in the last series of LWT's *Blind Date*. But when Gary (30) turned round, he discovered a queue of people wanting *his* autograph too!

Gary, whose date was a day out to Gleneagles with Helen, said later: "Powerful business, the old telly".

Michael Grade was tonight unavailable for comment.

### PROPERTY NEWS

A steep rise in property prices was feared today, after it was announced that Dave of Cambridge, who appeared on the first ever edition of *Blind Date*, and his fiancée, Mandy, had bought a house to live in after they are married.

Mandy, also of Cambridge, was so taken with Dave when she saw him on the show in November 1985, that she asked around, discovered who he was, and finally fixed up a real Blind Date with him. Since then, romance has blossomed.

A spokesman for the National

(cont. Back Page)

### BLIND DATE SPOTTERS' CLUB

Sightings of people who have been on BLIND DATE have come in from Tenerife (Gary), Mallorca (Sarah), Italy (Edith) and – in the lead so far – New Zealand (Philip).

Why don't you see how many Blind Daters you can spot? All you need is a pair of binoculars, a good field guide and some

(cont. Back Page)

### JUST FANCY THAT!

The people in Janet's office were eager to hear about her Blind Date, so she was telling them all about it, when one of the Sales team who had only joined them a few weeks before piped up and said "Where did you say you went on your date?"

"Punting in Oxford" said Janet.

"Oh, that was my brother you went with" came the amazing reply!

## BOY (25) EXPELLED FROM HOME
### Ends up in Drinking Den

Now, at last, the story can be told – and the sensational headline above explained.

The night young Mark of Halifax appeared on BLIND DATE, his mother, unable to bear the prospect of watching the show with him beside her, threw him out of the house.

Naturally, he was shattered. For what seemed like hours, he wandered the streets of Halifax, not knowing what to do.

At last, in his own words, "I decided to get it over with. If I'd made a prat of myself, the sooner I found out the better".

Courageously, he walked into his local – to discover all the chairs facing the TV set. The show had just finished. As Mark entered, everyone in the pub burst into spontaneous cheering. At that point, Mark said

(cont. Back Page)

### A MODEL START

Sizzling Sarah (22) is certainly stepping out as a result of her appearance last year on *Blind Date*. Ever since she got up and wiggled her bottom as a bunny girl, she's had more than enough to rabbit about! Her modelling career has taken off, and she hopes one day to be a TV presenter. So, look out Cilla! The girl who wiggled her bottom may soon be wiggling all the way to the top!

## THE SHEILA SHREW COLUMN

### TRACY TO WED MANDY SENSATION

Is the world going crazy, or is it me? What sort of country are we living in, when two people called "Tracy" and "Mandy" can become engaged to be married?!

OK – so "Tracy" is a fella, and appeared on *Blind Date* last year.

OK – so he met Mandy at the very first interview he went to for that programme, and liked her so much that he kept in touch afterwards.

OK – so they've been going out together for 18 months now.

But, if they *do* decide to get married, may I offer one suggestion? Just for once, wouldn't it be a good idea if the one to change his/her name at the wedding was not the *bride*, but the *groom*?

From "Tracy" to – may I suggest? – something like "Ron"?

Then silly old bats like myself wouldn't get over-excited about nothing any more.
\*\*\*

Is the world going stark, raving bonkers, or is it me?

Now I hear that one of the girl contestants on the new series of *Blind Date* is called "Ron"!

OK – so I'm a daft old biddy.

But would it be totally out of place to ask "Ron" to change her name as soon as possible to – may I suggest? – "Tracy"?

Then we'd *all* know where we were.

*Except Mandy!*

### "MIRACLE" IN MIDLANDS

Claims that the congregation at a Midlands cathedral has swelled in numbers since the daughter of the Dean appeared on *Blind Date* last September received a cautious welcome from Lambeth Palace tonight.

But a Roman Catholic spokesman commenting on the reports, said: "If true, this puts the Catholic Church at a considerable disadvantage. None of our priests have daughters, although we are

(cont. Back Page)

**SECOND DATE:** Last year, when they came back from their Blind Date to Champagne, Philip promised Mary he'd take her on another trip – this time round North Wales in one of his hire cars. Now, a year later, he's kept his promise. But what happened to the car, Phil?

### Travel Feature . . . PARIS

Is Paris the most romantic city in the world? A lot of Blind Daters seem to think so. Take Peter (26) from Northern Ireland, who appears in the current series. While staying in London for the recording of his show, he met an American who said to him "You must meet my daughter". He did – and the two of them got on so well, the father invited Peter to accompany the family to Paris! So ... do we have a romance? All Peter would tell the BLIND DATE team on his return was "You gotta right result. I may not have been picked – but you gotta right result!"

Also a Paris-lover is pert 23 year old Fiona from East Anglia. Talking on the sofa with Cilla and her Blind Date Allen, Fiona joked "We're going on a romantic weekend for two in Paris next week". They never did – but since then people haven't stopped asking her in a meaningful manner "Did you enjoy Paris?" Fiona says she's now utterly fed up with it!

George from Cambridge *did* go to Paris, with Edith from Rochdale. Now every time Paris appears on TV, he rings her up for a natter. "She does most of the talking!" quips ex-bus-inspector George. But his Blind Date has undoubtedly given him a new lease of life. Before it, he says, he was a lonely man. Now strangers greet him in the street, and he has got to know one of his neighbours much, much better. "I shall definitely be watching the next series with her. It's tea for two now" says George with a glint in his eye. Paris certainly turned out to be a romantic city for him!

### "CHIPMUNK" DENIES ELOPEMENT

by our Tittle-Tattle Correspondent

A grey and drawn Mandy, also known as "Chipmunk", of Freckleton, near Blackpool, emerged from hiding today to deny rumours sweeping Lancashire of her involvement with the man who chose her on *Blind Date*, Peter of Oxford.

"It's all a ghastly mistake" she told me, fighting back floods of giggles. "A friend of mine overheard a woman in a local hairdresser's saying that Peter and I had eloped and got married. Just because we went climbing on our date,

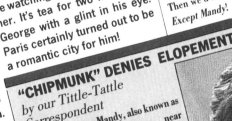

it doesn't mean Peter was the type to put a ladder up to a girl's window to steal her away!"

Since Mandy appeared on the show last autumn, she has been recognised everywhere she goes. "In Blackpool," she told me, "a man stared at me for a long time, and at last shouted 'You were in *The Price is Right*! Come on Down!'"

But the big question remains. If Peter (26) really had put a ladder up to Mandy's window and invited her to elope, would she have stayed put, or would she have ... "Come on Down"?

All the
People
who have
ever…

...appeared on Blind Date so far

## THE CLASSROOM GAME

**Rules**

1   Teacher plays Cilla.

2   Everybody submits three questions and the teacher chooses the best boy's and the best girl's.

3   The teacher then reads out the questions, and everyone in the class of the opposite sex to the picker writes down their answers.

4   The answers are then collected, and the teacher chooses the best three sets and reads them out.

5   The pickers choose which pickee they prefer and then must spend the lunch-hour with their choices.

6   They report back after lunch and tell the class what they have discovered about their "date" that they didn't know before.

## THE CARD GAME

**Rules**

1   This is a game for 8 or more players. Ideally, there should be an equal number of boys and girls, but, if the numbers are unbalanced, the larger group must be the pickees. The more players there are, the merrier.

2   The following rules are written with the girls as pickers, and the boys as pickees, but they work, or course, just as well the other way about. It is assumed throughout that there are 4 girls and 4 boys.

3   Equipment required: small filing cards (all the same colour); felt-tip

# PARTY BLIND DATE

**Well, now you've seen how we do it, how would you like to have a go at Blind Date yourself?** There are three elements to the game you have to organize – the question-and-answer session, the date and the reporting back afterwards. It's not really essential to report back to anyone if you don't want to – the blind date can be just for the fun of the couple who go on it. In fact, there's no need even to have a "date", as such. You could play the first part of the game simply to determine who sits next to whom at a big family meal like Christmas lunch. Anyway, however you play it – good luck, and have fun!

What is this picker to do? She has 3 blue cards, but the thought of a Blind Date with the writer of those answers is too ghastly to contemplate. So she will get rid of her blues as soon as she can, and hope to collect more reds and greens. And, of course, there are two other colours that might be even more attractive. She has a long way to go!

pens (all different colours).

4   The pickers and pickees are separated. Between them the pickers devise 5 questions (only 3 if there are 7 pickees or more). These are written individually onto the cards, one set of 5 for each pickee. Thus with 4 pickees, there are 20 cards.

5   Each pickee is given a set and, using a coloured pen of his own choice, prints on each card an answer to the question thereon. The cards are collected up, shuffled and dealt out to the pickers, each receiving 5 cards.

6   The object of the game is

to collect a complete set of answers all written in the same colour and win a Blind Date with the writer of them. A secondary object is to avoid getting landed with the wally, the wimp or the poser (or the female equivalents). This isn't so easy.

7   Play begins with the picker on the left of the dealer giving any card in her hand that she wants to get rid of to the picker on *her* left, who must take it and give her a card from her own hand in exchange. The second picker then does a similar swap with the next picker, and so on round the table. This ensures

that at all times every picker has 5 cards in her hand.

8   As soon as a picker has collected a complete set of 5 cards from the same pickee, and *provided she wants to*, she shouts "Blind Date" and wins the game. The writer of the cards is called in and the couple are introduced to each other.

9   The remaining players then continue the game until another "Blind Date" is called. The process is continued until only 2 pickers remain. Each of these then has to go out with whoever wrote the majority of cards they are left holding.

# TA-RA FOR NOW!

ANSWERS TO "WHO SAID WHAT?" on pages 30-31

Peter's Question: Left 3, Middle 1, Right 2
David's Question: Left 3, Middle 2, Right 1
Clare's Question: Left 2, Middle 1, Right 3
Jan's Question: Left 2, Middle 3, Right 1

BLIND DATE IS A TEAM EFFORT AND WHAT PEOPLE MAY NOT REALISE IS THAT EVERYTHING IS DONE BEFORE I APPEAR ON THE SCENE RIGHT DOWN TO MAKING PEOPLE FEEL AT HOME AND CREATING THAT PARTY ATMOSPHERE. I'M JUST THE ICING ON THE CAKE! SO A BIG THANK YOU TO THE BLIND DATE TEAM ... AND OF COURSE, TO THE HUNDREDS OF GOOD SPORTS WHO COME AND TAKE PART IN BLIND DATE WE ALSO SAY THANK YOU – WITHOUT YOU WE WOULDN'T HAVE A SHOW.

PRODUCER Gill Stribling-Wright, EXECUTIVE PRODUCER Marcus Plantin, DIRECTOR Terry Kinane, PROGRAMME ASSOCIATE Chris Miller, ASSOCIATE PRODUCERS Philip Livingstone, Kevin Roast, RESEARCHERS Rosetta Bain, Anne Gilchrist, Andrea Haines, PRODUCTION ASSISTANTS Hazel Allinson, Laura Brown, STAGE MANAGER John Gregory, ADDITIONAL MATERIAL Vince Powell, PRODUCTION SECRETARIES Nony Barrow, Karen Walsh, PRODUCTION MANAGER Myra Hersh, SET DESIGNER Richard Dunn, GRAPHICS Peter Johnson, COSTUME DESIGNER Stephen Adnitt, MAKE UP SUPERVISOR Wendy Brown, Hilary Martin, SOUND SUPERVISOR Mark McLoughlin, LIGHTING DIRECTOR Paul Stripp, CAMERAS Dave Taylor & Crew 7, VISION MIXER Barbara Hicks, FLOOR MANAGER Simon Wallace, VIDEOTAPE EDITORS Wink Hackman, Clayton Parker, Graham Sisson, AUTOCUE Gretal Plumley, MUSIC Laurie Holloway, THE VOICE OF Graham Skidmore, WARM-UP Bill Martin, PHOTOGRAPHERS Simon Farrell, Tony Russell, Mike Vaughan, PICTURE PUBLICITY Shane Chapman, Mandy Mills, PRESS OFFICER Rita Borman.

**1986**
DIRECTOR John Gorman, ASSOCIATE PRODUCERS Sean Murphy, Robert Randell, RESEARCHERS Juliet Blake, Helen Wright, MAKE UP SUPERVISOR Sabina Cowen, LIGHTING DIRECTOR Bryan Love, CAMERAS Lisle Middleditch & Crew 6, VISION MIXER Paul Wheeler, PHOTOGRAPHER Steve Morley.

**1985**
ASSOCIATE PRODUCER Michael Longmire, RESEARCHERS Paul Lewis, Juliet Winstone, PRODUCTION ASSISTANT Carole de Caux, STAGE MANAGER Jane Denholm, ADDITIONAL MATERIAL Colin Edmonds, PRODUCTION MANAGER Mike Ayres, GRAPHICS Chris Sharp, SOUND SUPERVISOR Graham Thor-Straten, LIGHTING DIRECTOR Teddy Fader.